Safe Sanctuaries
in a Virtual World

Safe Sanctuaries in a Virtual World

Joy Thornburg Melton and Michelle L. Foster

DISCIPLESHIP RESOURCES

PO BOX 340003 • NASHVILLE, TN 37203-0003
www.discipleshipresources.org

Copyright © 2014 Joy Thornburg Melton and Michelle L. Foster. All rights reserved.

No part of this book may be reproduced in any form whatsoever, print or electronic, without written permission, except in the case of brief quotations embodied in critical articles or reviews and those pages designated "Reproducible." For information regarding rights and permissions, contact Discipleship Resources, P.O. Box 340003, Nashville, TN 37203-0003.

The publisher is glad to grant permission to reproduce the sample forms in the Sample Forms section of this book.

At the time of publication all websites referenced in this book were valid. However, due to the fluid nature of the Internet, some addresses may have changed, or the content may no longer be relevant.

Safe Sanctuaries® is a trademark owned by the General Board of Discipleship of The United Methodist Church, Nashville, Tennessee. All rights reserved.

Unless otherwise noted, scripture quotations are from the New Revised Standard Version Bible, copyright © 1989 National Council of the Churches of Christ in the United States of America. Used by permission. All rights reserved.

Scripture quotations noted THE MESSAGE are from *THE MESSAGE*. Copyright © 1993, 1994, 1996, 2000, 2001, 2002. Used by permission of NavPress Publishing Group.

Scripture quotations noted NIV are from The Holy Bible, New International Version® NIV® Copyright © 1973, 1978, 1984, 2011 by Biblica, Inc.™ Used by permission. All rights reserved worldwide.

Cover design by Joey McNair

Library of Congress Control Number: 2014931197

ISBNs:
Print 978-0-88177-630-0
Mobi 978-0-88177-647-8
Epub 978-0-88177-648-5

Printed in the United States of America

DR630

To Marc, Michael, and Pearson Foster, with gratitude for their support, endless conversations, love, and encouragement throughout this journey. Michael and Pearson, may this simple offering remind you of the power of pursuing your dreams and the goodness of God as you constantly seek God's direction throughout all of life.

—Michelle L. Foster

With all my love to David and Kathryn Melton, my family.

—Joy Thornburg Melton

Contents

Chapter 1: Foundations and Pillars 9
    Ecclesiology 10
    Theology 11
    Covenantal Relationship 11
    Liability 12
    Our Current Situation 13
    Boundaries 16
    Sacred Space 19

Chapter 2: Application of Law to the Life of the Church 21
    Copyright and the Digital Age 21
    Selection, Hiring, and Supervision 27

Chapter 3: Basic Procedures for Ministry in a Virtual World 43
    A Story of Power, Pain, and Technology 43
    Cell Phones 45
    Social Media 50

Chapter 4: Pornography and Obscenity 59
    The Gift of Sex 59
    Pornography 60
    What the Laws Say about Pornography and Obscenity 65

Chapter 5: Specialized Contexts of Ministry—FAQs 71
    Camping and Retreat Ministries 71

Safe Sanctuaries in a Virtual World

    Campus Ministries   73
    Preschool and After-school Ministries   74
    Sports and Leisure Ministries   75
    Pastoral Moves and Social Media   76
    Visitor and New Member Assimilation Ministries   79

Chapter 6: Training and Response 81

    Opening Worship   81
    Introductory Information   82
    Closing Worship   84
    A Model for Response   85
    Continuing Ministry of Response   90

Sample Forms 95

    Sample Social Media Use Policy for Employees   95
    Sample Social Media Use Policy for Volunteers   97
    Sample Youth Ministry Leadership Covenant   99
    Sample Authorization Form for Photo and Video Usage   101
    Sample Pastoral Ministry Covenant Regarding the Use of Facebook
       and Other Social Media   102

Sources and Resources 103

    Books and Publications   103
    Helpful Websites   105
    Newsletters   106
    Blogs   106
    United Methodist Resources   106

Notes 109

About the Authors 111

Chapter 1

Foundations and Pillars

> I therefore, the prisoner in the Lord, beg you to lead a life worthy of the calling to which you have been called, with all humility and gentleness, with patience, bearing with one another in love, making every effort to maintain the unity of the Spirit in the bond of peace.
> —Ephesians 4:1-3

This book addresses the ministry challenges that have arisen and will arise as we embrace the reality of the changing face of ministry in our twenty-first-century technological age. Technology is easy to access and use in nearly every aspect of our lives. It is rare to meet someone who is not familiar with a computer, doesn't own a cell phone, or at the very least hasn't taken pictures using a digital camera. With every passing day, technology is becoming more user-friendly and intuitive. Usually not cost-prohibitive, it is streamlining the way we work and interact with one another and the world around us. The speed with which technology evolves is also a sign that electronic devices are going to become more and more integrated into our ways of living and being.

When originally conceived, the vision for the content of this book was that the information would be directed toward clergy. It didn't take long for us to realize the need for this conversation to include all of God's people because we all are looking for guidance and direction in being faithful to the witness of Jesus Christ, even as we live out our lives in the midst of an ever-changing world. This resource is developed intentionally for clergy, church staff (paid and unpaid), and Safe Sanctuaries Leadership Teams. While the entirety of this book is not a "a one size fits all," it has been written to offer best practices, suggestions, recommendations, and ideas for implementation that are easily tailored for your particular context and size of ministry.

Holding conversations about ethics, especially related to technology, is often difficult for many. Here are some of the reasons why:

- The scope of technological knowledge varies greatly from one person to the next.

Safe Sanctuaries in a Virtual World

- There is a wide gap of variation when we begin to try to define what is ethical and unethical regarding technology, especially when we use laws to try to distinguish the boundaries.

- Technology is used in a wide variety and complexity of ministry settings and situations.

- This conversation, or any conversation, may not provide us all the answers that we need now or will need in the future regarding the subject of technology and the church.

Even with all of this in mind, we begin the conversation.

Ethics are the moral principles that give shape to the way we conduct ourselves as individuals and groups of people. In this particular conversation ethics can be further defined as guiding principles that give shape to the ways we as Christians will engage with and use technology in our personal and ministry settings that honor and glorify Christ.

The foundation for all that follows is this: **Ethics in regard to technology is a matter of ecclesiology, theology, covenantal relationship, and, last, a matter of liability for God's people.**

Ecclesiology

Ecclesiology is the study of the church. The biblical understanding of ecclesiology defines church as a community of believers united in and through the saving work of Jesus Christ. Church is not a building or a place. Ethics as a matter of ecclesiology is about being "church" to one another. Our biblical understanding of church is that of a sacred community where trust, love, grace, and forgiveness are offered to one another in Christlike servanthood. Paul, especially in his letter to the church at Ephesus, bravely and articulately speaks of church: "Speaking the truth in love, we must grow up in every way into him who is the head, into Christ, from whom the whole body, joined and knit together by every ligament with which it is equipped, as each part is working properly, promotes the body's growth in building itself up in love" (Ephesians 4:15-16). Ecclesiology in its most basic form is about the ways we live out our relationships with God and God's people. The apostle Paul, in writing to the church in Ephesus, offers practical directions for life and living to those who bear the name of Christ:

> As a prisoner for the Lord, then, I urge you to live a life worthy of the calling you have received. Be completely humble and gentle; be patient, bearing with one another in love. Make every effort to keep the unity of the Spirit through the bond of peace. There is one body and one Spirit—just as you were called to one hope when you were called—one Lord, one faith, one baptism; one God and Father of all, who is over all and through all and in all. (Ephesians 4:1-6, NIV)

Paul is reminding us that we are called to lead lives worthy of those who bear Christ's name to all generations.

Chapter 1: Foundations and Pillars

Theology

United Methodist theology, as expressed and experienced through the sacrament of holy baptism, initiates us into God's holy church, incorporates us into God's mighty acts of salvation, and calls us to be witnesses for all the world to see. Our lives are a response and a reflection of God's goodness. Because we are one body, Christ's body, we have the responsibility to maintain the unity of the Spirit. Paul is reminding us that through our baptisms we are all made one in Christ. We are called to be one body, to maintain the unity of the Spirit, and to live with one another by practicing the virtues of love, justice, healing, compassion, mercy, respect, forgiveness, and accountability. These virtues were exemplified for us through the life of Jesus Christ. As brothers and sisters with him, we are called to live out these same virtuous characteristics, which we often call the fruit of the Spirit: "love, joy, peace, patience, kindness, generosity, faithfulness, gentleness, and self-control" (Galatians 5:22-23). The way of discipleship is active. It is a constant process of being trained in God's ways. Not only are we commanded to know the commandments of God (Exodus 20:1-17 and Deuteronomy 5:6-21); we are called to live them out, as we have seen exemplified in Christ Jesus.

To be the body of Christ, we must share in a common vision, practice, and understanding of what it means to embody Christ for the world. This does not mean, however, that we must agree on everything. To share a common vision, practice, and understanding is to hold in mutual agreement a core set of beliefs and practices that each member of the community then exemplifies and lives out of based on the ways in which Christ has gifted him or her for service. For Paul, this meant the cultivation of humility and gentleness, patience, love, faithfulness, and peace. We are not simply witnesses to the sacrament of holy baptism; we are participants in every baptism that happens before our eyes. As members of God's church, we commit "with God's help to so order our lives after the example of Christ, that we will surround each baptized person with steadfast love, so that they may be established in the faith, and confirmed and strengthened in the way that leads to life eternal."[1]

Covenantal Relationship

The work of "bearing with one another in love" (Ephesians 4:2, NIV) is about being in authentic relationship with one another. The work of community and church is about encouraging and nurturing God's Spirit within one another. Relationships are about love, gratitude, and forgiveness. The work of authentic relationships rooted in Jesus Christ is expressed and experienced through participation in corporate worship and personal acts of spiritual discipline, growing inwardly and serving outwardly, and being the church to the world. The work of being the church also means clearly establishing boundaries, principles, and guidelines by which we will hold one another accountable to unity in the Spirit of God.

The word *ethics* is a noun used to describe a system of moral principles. The work of ethics and ethical behavior is about covenantal relationship with one another. A covenant is a sacred agreement to serve as Christ's representatives in the world with God and with others who bear Christ's name. Covenants are initiated by God for God's

> To be the body of Christ, we must share in a common vision, practice, and understanding of what it means to embody Christ for the world.

good purposes to be accomplished. Our participation in God's covenant is our "yes" to being led and shaped by God for God's kingdom and purposes. Some call this a response to God's saving invitation, others call it justifying grace as we recognize and claim God's grace that has already been present in our lives, and for others this is their commitment to go in the direction of God.

Steve Manskar, in his book *Opening Ourselves to Grace: The Means of Grace and Discipleship*, speaks about grace and accountability in this way: "With [the acceptance of grace] comes accountability. . . . We must live by God's household rules. . . .The life that God gives cannot be lived alone. It must be lived in a community (the church) of love and forgiveness. . . . Grace is universal . . . none are excluded from God's love, compassion, and justice."[2] Covenantal relationship involves all of God's people. Ordination is only one example of a sacred covenant to which some are invited to enter into with God and with the church to serve as servant leaders among God's people. All are called to be ministers; our baptism incorporates us into the priesthood of all believers. Ministry is about authentic relationships that are bound in sacred and holy trust through the life, death, and resurrection of Jesus Christ. We are in ministry to offer Christ to others. Accountability is the way in which we honor the sacred and the vulnerable in every person. A covenantal relationship with one another involves growing, loving, encouraging, and nurturing one another as parts of Christ's body. Covenantal relationships are God's way of encouraging us to prune, pluck, shape, and remold one another with Christ's love in order that we might become more and more Christlike throughout the totality of our lives. Remember, it is ethics that give shape to the guiding principles of a person or group of people. Guiding principles indicate to us what is acceptable as well as what is not acceptable as a part of a particular group. Christian ethics are what offers shape to the guiding principles of those who bear Christ's name and endeavor to witness, through word, action, and thought, the love, grace, and mercy of Jesus the Christ. These Christian ethics help us to determine what is Christlike and what is outside the boundaries of Christlike living.

Liability

Many times we try to reduce ethics to a matter of liability. There is a prevailing belief that we require education around sexual harassment, appropriate touching and intimacy, inclusive language, appropriate use of technology, and so on to avoid the possibility of lawsuits and major financial payouts. The reality is that from the perspective of integrity in the faith community, financial and legal liabilities are the least of our concerns. As the church universal, our primary focus is and should be our authentic witness for Jesus Christ to the world as the living embodiment of Christ right here, right now. Legal issues and liabilities are important, without a doubt. Nevertheless, the primary questions should be: Are we really being the light of Christ to a dark and hurting world? Is the church giving direction and leading the charge when it comes to modeling the appropriate use of technology? Or is the church simply jumping on the train of current culture and whatever is the prevailing thought of the day? These are the foundational questions that call us to remember that we are God's people, called to be Christ's witnesses in the ways we worship, speak, and conduct ourselves in and with the world.

Chapter 1: Foundations and Pillars

As God's people we have to acknowledge and accept that our actions have consequences. Good actions and decisions produce good, healthy outcomes. Poor decisions and actions often produce negative consequences and harm to ourselves, other individuals, and groups of people. The harm that occurs, whether physical, spiritual, or emotional, creates a liability for which the individual and/or the church is responsible. Because we live in a society in which great value is placed on money, the restoration process of a liable action or set of actions is usually realized through large amounts of money being awarded by the court system after a lengthy trial. Once an indiscretion has occurred, the goal is often to mitigate legal actions and financial settlements. The true liability of which we speak, however, is not about money or insurance investigations or timely courtroom proceedings. The true liability that we are trying to address is that of a spiritual and theological nature.

> We are called to be God's church, in this time, in our particular place in this world, for all with whom we will engage.

The actions of one have great consequences and affect all: "If one member suffers, all suffer together with it; if one member [of the body] is honored, all rejoice together with it. Now you are the body of Christ and individually members of it" (1 Corinthians 12:26-27). When Christ's body is fractured because of indiscretions, poor decisions, and overall disregard for unity in the Holy Spirit, God's people are hurt. Trust is destroyed. Christian integrity is called into question. The example of Christ is marred. Those seeking the church as a place of refuge instead find it a place of pain and hurt. Questions, confusion, and concern take the place of peace, joy, and unity. Utilizing technology within the context of ministry comes with risks. Some of the risks are known and others are still unknown. The liability that we carry with us as we use technology is that some may use it inappropriately, thereby harming the unity of Christ's body, the church. The liability is greatly reduced, however, when we "[bear] with one another in love" (Ephesians 4:2) and practice mutual accountability with one another.

Remember, **ethics in regard to technology is a matter of ecclesiology, theology, covenantal relationship, and, last, a matter of liability for God's people.** We are called to be God's church, in this time, in our particular place in this world, for all with whom we will engage. Our theological understanding of mutual care, support, and accountability brings us into covenantal relationship with one another and with God, thereby greatly reducing the liability that exists for God's people to cause fractures in the unity of the Holy Spirit.

It is because of this that we, as Christians, together journey into the world of technology.

Our Current Situation

Our twenty-first-century world is flooded with a myriad of ways to stay in contact with one another. From e-mails to cell phones, social networking sites to blogs, video chats to virtual worlds, we are constantly connected without regard to geography, time zone, or depth of relationship. We as humans are made in the image of the triune God, and we long for companionship and connection with one another. Technology and its ease of use fuels our hunger for connection, relationships, and companionship. The problem is that for the first time in human history we have the ability to develop

Safe Sanctuaries in a Virtual World

and cultivate relationships with people whom we have never met, whose identities we cannot immediately verify, and whom we may never see face-to-face.

Our understandings of human behavior are based in real-life situations and interactions with one another. Technology and the entire virtual world now skew the personal interactions we have come to rely on when communicating with another person. The screen of a computer, smart phone, or tablet greatly reduces our ability to observe facial expressions, hear the tone of voice when a statement is offered, observe the nonverbal body cues given in personal interactions, or verify the information that is offered regarding the person's identity, character, and intent.

Families have guidelines and norms for members' interacting with one another. Relationships with colleagues include a prescribed standard of behavior and set of norms. Within friendships we have normative standards and guidelines related to the way we interact with one another. Communities have social norms and acceptable behaviors. Teachers in classrooms develop class rules and standards for engagement; even states and nations develop laws and statutes that govern the way people are in relationship with one another. So too, relationships in a virtual world need a set of standards, guidelines, and rules in which we operate. Many of these rules and boundaries are offered to us through the "host" organization—be that a social networking site, a cell phone provider, or even the government.

As people set apart for the work of ministry in the name of Christ, we must continue to heed the words of scripture and apply the principles that we glean from the Holy Spirit in order to lead lives worthy of our calling. Beyond the established rules and norms given to us by the world, we are called to consider the additional practices of ethical behavior that are congruent with our understanding of God and our relationship with God and God's people. The boundaries and guidelines that we create for face-to-face interactions must also serve as signposts or benchmarks for use on our journey into the world of virtual reality and technology. Our relationships, be they with our next-door neighbors or people halfway around the world whom we may never meet face-to-face, must remain grounded in our scriptural understanding of our calling, the covenantal relationship we are in with God and all Christians, the practice of participation in the priesthood of all believers, and the vows of ordination and licensing that we accepted when we responded to Christ's call in our lives.

For the majority of us, our use of multimedia, in one form or another, aids our ability to proclaim the good news of Jesus Christ. When we speak of technology we are including cell phones and all their capabilities, the Internet, social networking sites, and even e-mails.

We are in contact with others in numerous ways throughout the day and night. As clergy and leaders in the church, people seek us out for comfort, advice, leadership, support, and spiritual growth. It is important for us to remember that these relationships are sacred gifts from God. Technology is a tool that we use to be in relationship with others. The use of technology is a privilege, and in using that privilege we must exercise responsibility.

Even as we engage in this conversation, we are aware of those among us whose lives are constantly and intrinsically connected with technology—and we are also aware of

Chapter 1: Foundations and Pillars

those on the other end of the spectrum who avoid technology and any use of it. The great majority of us live somewhere in the middle of these two extremes. Technology is an ever-present reality regardless of how we feel about it. Therefore, it is incumbent upon us to understand how people use technology and how people's abuse of it causes harm to themselves and others.

Cell phones, the Internet, and social media have proved to be helpful and useful tools in our ministry. Technology

- helps us communicate in real or near real time;
- provides an avenue to disseminate a lot of information in a very short amount of time; and
- is generally readily available and spans large geographical areas without a lot of problems.

Multimedia usage is an everyday part of our culture. It is a mechanism we use to engage in ministry and equip others for discipleship and ministry in the world. In our use of technology, it is imperative that we continue to consider the boundaries we establish, the ways we respect other people's boundaries, and the dynamic that exists when engaging in conversation with a person who is not physically in front of us.

Two of the biggest problems facing the church today in the area of technology are (1) online sexualized behavior; and (2) the use and abuse of pornography found online. Both of these stem from a third problem, which is inappropriate personal and interpersonal boundaries. We are living in a society in which cultural norms and values are quickly shifting from a communal sense of right and wrong to a more individualized "me-centered" society where anything goes, and to each their own. It is becoming more and more difficult to determine and define communal boundaries. Because of the eroding nature of community and the continual rise of the "Just do it" culture, many people are growing up without any sense of appropriate personal and communal boundaries. As leaders in the church, we are highly shaped by the world and our experiences in it. Given our desire to stay relevant and of the world while not in the world, we too are struggling to understand what is right and what is wrong, where the proverbial line in the sand is between the two, and the ways we intentionally and unintentionally cross that line.

More and more church leaders are struggling with appropriate boundaries related to the use of multimedia in ministry and relationships. Boundary-crossing can be as simple as the tone and character of our e-mails and actions shifting from professional and business-oriented information sharing to more personal and informal sharing. It is easy to forget that our written words are just as powerful, if not more powerful, than the words we speak. When we change our Facebook statuses to reflect our frustration with some unnamed church member who has just stormed into our offices; or we tweet or blog about how tired we are, how unappreciative our spouses are of all our hard work, and how taken for granted we are as leaders in the church, we have crossed personal and professional boundaries. We begin to walk on a very slippery slope when we do not have healthy boundaries in place concerning the use of technology. The slope continues to become more slippery when we begin to engage in relationships online.

Notes

Boundaries

> I'm single-minded in pursuit of you;
> don't let me miss the road signs you've posted.
> I've banked your promises in the vault of my heart
> so I won't sin myself bankrupt.
> Be blessed, God;
> train me in your ways of wise living.
> I'll transfer to my lips
> all the counsel that comes from your mouth;
> I delight far more in what you tell me about living
> than in gathering a pile of riches.
> I ponder every morsel of wisdom from you,
> I attentively watch how you've done it.
> I relish everything you've told me of life,
> I won't forget a word of it.
> —Psalm 119:10-16 (The Message)

The reality is that we, like the psalmist, want to do what God desires. Yet, as children of God and members of the priesthood of all believers, we often struggle to know what is right; we wrestle with issues of boundaries, integrity, character, and self-worth.

Boundaries are the "road signs" posted to guide and direct us in wise living. Boundaries are limits, set by others and by ourselves, for engaging and interacting with the world. Parents set boundaries for children regarding bedtime, TV watching, diet, personal care, and the list goes on. Teachers establish boundaries in their classrooms often called "class rules." Cities and states establish boundaries for us regarding safe travel speeds, child restraint seats, prescribed drugs, and so on. We often establish boundaries for ourselves regarding what we eat, where we go, what we wear, the relationships of which we are a part, what types of medical intervention we want in any given situation, and how our bodies will be handled after death. Boundaries are one way we define where our individual rights, privileges, and power end and those of other people begin.

In my own primary setting of ministry, I (Michelle) spend a lot of time with those who are hospitalized, homebound, or facing life transitions and crisis situations. Healthy boundaries keep me from being overwhelmed by others' stories and needs. Boundaries remind me that while I can appropriately offer care and comfort, guidance and spiritual nurture, their problems or situations are not mine to carry.

Words and actions that betray the sacred in another person are boundary violations. Violations are not just about stepping over the proverbial line in the sand. That would focus on breaking a rule, a norm, or a principle. Boundary violations are also about the resulting harm that is inflicted upon another person. The harm can be physical, psychological, spiritual, or emotional.

The confounding situation that we face as ministry leaders is the fact that we are crossing societal boundaries all the time:

Chapter 1: Foundations and Pillars

- ☑ We often call people at their private residences or on their personal cell phones.
  Think about how upset we get when our dinners are interrupted by a telemarketer.

- ☑ We visit and conduct business in people's homes.
  Most other professionals and businesses conduct business in offices and public places.

- ☑ In the most vulnerable times of life, we are present and seen as trusted leaders. We are often present during births, deaths, weddings, tragedies, and serious medical-care situations.
  Most professionals, while they address legal needs and necessary care during these vulnerable times of life, do not engage in emotional and spiritual caregiving.

When we are not clear with ourselves about boundary setting and the ways we can appropriately and healthfully care for others, these types of situations allow boundaries to become blurred and sacred trust to be compromised.

As leaders and caregivers, we often go into ministry for the intimacy of the situations; to be able to be with and help others in the tough places of their lives. This is especially true for clergy in the denominational context, Stephen Ministers, hospice volunteers, youth counselors, and paid church staff. This truth exists even more broadly and extends to pastors, evangelical speakers, and prophets, among others in the nondenominational context. We want to help people find meaning as children of God. The demands of and the situations of ministry in which we find ourselves often make it difficult to stay balanced and to be aware of the true needs we are addressing.

We are constantly receiving mixed messages from multiple sources, including ourselves, regarding how to best handle our ministries. Even seminary and other training events send us mixed messages. Sometimes we are told not to be physically close to anyone. Don't hug anyone, and certainly don't become friends with anyone in a group you are leading. In another breath we are told that people long for relationships and human contact. We are encouraged to always be available, to share intimately in others' journeys of pain and joy, and to provide human contact, especially as it pertains to hugs and holding hands.

Ministry is complex. Complexity beckons for clear boundaries so that the sacred in every person is honored and valued. The task before us is to examine intentionally, often, and honestly our boundaries so that we can stay healthy in our lives and relationships.

Terms Describing Sexual Misconduct

As we begin diving into this world of boundaries and looking for clear guidance in the midst of tough ministry situations, it is important to examine several words and phrases that we often use when we begin to engage in any conversation about sexual ethics. Given that two of the three greatest problems facing the church are focused around issues of sexuality, it is important to be familiar with all these terms and the definitions associated with each. These definitions also apply to the use of technology both off-line and online.

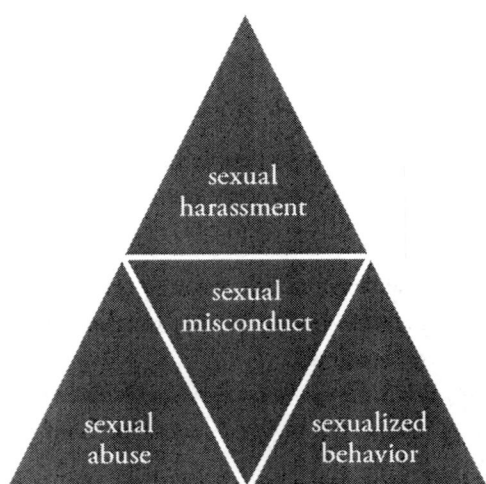

Sexual misconduct is any unwanted sexual or gender-directed behavior by either a layperson or a clergyperson within a ministerial relationship. I have placed it in the center of the triangle because it can include child abuse, adult sexual abuse, harassment, sexual assault, sexualized verbal comments or visuals, unwelcome advances or touching, use of sexualized material, stalking, sexual abuse without capacity to consent, or even misuse of the pastoral or ministerial position by using sexualized conduct to take advantage of the vulnerability of another. There are certain aspects of sexual misconduct that are also considered to be criminal behavior in some nations, states, and communities. The definitions below represent the United Methodist tradition. Similar definitions can be found in other denominations and in the laws at both the federal and state levels.

Sexual harassment is a form of sexual misconduct that is defined in ¶1611 of the Social Principles of The United Methodist Church as found in *The United Methodist Book of Discipline—2012*. Sexual harassment is any unwanted sexual or gender-directed behavior within a pastoral, employment, ministerial, mentor, or colleague relationship that is so severe or pervasive that it alters the conditions of employment or volunteer work or unreasonably interferes with the employee's or volunteer's performance by creating a hostile, offensive environment. Sexual harassment can include unwanted sexual jokes, repeated advances, touching, or comments that insult and/or degrade or sexually exploit women, men, elderly persons, children, or youth.

Sexual abuse is a form of sexual misconduct that occurs when a person within a ministerial role of leadership (lay or clergy, pastor, educator, counselor, youth leader, or another position of leadership) engages in sexual contact or sexualized behavior with a congregant, client, employee, student, staff member, coworker, or volunteer. Sexual abuse includes coerced or forced sexual contact, sexual interaction or contact with children or youth, and sexual exhibitionism or any display of sexual visuals or pornography.

Sexualized behavior is any behavior that communicates sexual interest and/or content. Examples include but are not limited to displaying sexually aggressive visual materials, use of pornography in church programs on or within church property, making sexual comments or innuendos about one's own or another person's body, touching another person's body, hair, or clothing, touching or rubbing oneself in the

Chapter 1: Foundations and Pillars

presence of another person, kissing, and sexual intercourse. Sexualized behavior can be a form of sexual misconduct when this behavior is unwanted by the recipient or witness, is a violation of society's or the church's law, breaks the sacred trust in the ministerial role, or violates the vows taken at membership or ordination.

Sacred Space

Ministry is often a confusing venture. The more we are aware of our words, thoughts, and actions, the more we are able to lovingly and appropriately care for ourselves and others. I think you might agree that boundaries in interpersonal relationships are sometimes tricky. I have one friend who loves to hug each time we see each other. Another friend is not a hugger. It has taken some time for us to come to an agreed-upon physical greeting and good-bye. This is not a statement about hugging. It is an example of the ways I have come to respect and value the sacred space of two different friends. A similar example might also be translated into the virtual world. I love taking pictures and capturing every moment of life. One friend, Emily, has no problem with my posting her picture on Facebook. Another friend, Jen, because of the nature of her job, does not want her picture posted. Emily and Jen are captured in pictures that are on my camera. It would be a boundary violation to continue to post pictures of Jen after she has asked me not to do so. The boundary violation would be not only because of the rule Jen has set. The violation would be because of the harm it would cause Jen, in her profession and within our friendship, for me not to respect her enough to honor her request for privacy.

We recognize that ministry is often a bewildering endeavor into uncharted territory, and that endeavor is now compounded with the indeterminate world of technology at our fingertips. In this book we have provided the latest statistics, as well as descriptions of best practices and some real-life situations, along with questions for reflection, as tools of guidance for ministry within and beyond the walls of the church.

Notes

Chapter 2
Application of Law to the Life of the Church

"What is written in the law? What do you read there?" [Jesus] answered, "You shall love the Lord your God with all your heart, and with all your soul, and with all your strength, and with all your mind; and your neighbor as yourself."

—Luke 10:26-27

Copyright and the Digital Age

At Perfection Church, the weekly worship bulletin is created and arranged to be consistent with and reflective of the theme or focus of worship for that particular day. The worship services are designed to be relevant and contemporary. It is customary for this church to use multimedia presentations in worship. They have a live band that leads the congregation in singing popular contemporary Christian music. (Many of the songs are currently being heard on the radio and come from popular contemporary Christian artists.) The lyrics to the songs are displayed on screens in the worship space. Sometimes different video clips from the Internet or movies are used to supplement the sermons, as is a variety of different images and photographs. It is also standard for the biblical text of the day to be displayed on the screen as it is read aloud to the congregation.

In light of the description of Perfection Church you've just read, answer the following questions:

- *Where do you see your context of ministry in this situation?*
- *Given what information and knowledge you currently possess about copyright and the use of information available online, where in this scenario would copyright permission need to be sought?*
- *What materials are available for public use without permission or any acknowledgment of the location/owner of the source?*

Moving from printed worship bulletins, hymnals in the pew racks, the same version of the Bible available for every person present, and a primarily auditory-focused worship service to a more integrative, multisensory, less-paper-producing way of worship

Safe Sanctuaries in a Virtual World

takes a lot of work. As leaders in the church, we have experienced, used, encouraged, and found comfort in a particular way of doing things, including worship. If we are honest with ourselves, we are also aware that this way of worship is quickly feeling and looking out-of-date, flat, and without relevance to those seeking to encounter the living God through our services of worship. In response, we are trying our very best to stay aware of the trends and technology that result in relevant shifts in the tools available for teaching and sharing the gospel of Jesus Christ, all the while expending a ton of time and energy to bring those tools into our ways and places of worship and growth.

Probably one of the most difficult areas for the church to consider involves the boundaries incumbent upon us to recognize and respect when it comes to utilizing information that is readily available to us on the Internet. The whole understanding of copyright law, copyright infringement, and fair use of copyrighted material is much more difficult to navigate when there are not books, copyright authorizations, and standard bibliographies attached or easily locatable for sources of the materials we are using. The biggest point to keep in mind is that ease of accessibility does not equate to free and public use.

This chapter is a starting point in understanding and navigating copyright law and the digital age. Simply stated, a copyright is an exclusive legal right given to an author, creator, or owner that protects against the unauthorized use of original works, concepts, and creations for a set period of time.

The term *owner* in this definition acknowledges that copyright often shifts from an original author or creator to another entity or person when someone purchases the creative product, design, or idea. "Owner" may also refer to a particular agency, entity, or business that one is working on behalf of as original works, concepts, or creations are brought to fruition. Some examples of this may be an article that is written or a photograph that is taken while working as an employee of a newspaper or other printed periodical. Many times in the music world there are shared or transferred copyrights of music. One person writes original words and music and then sells it to a publishing company. Both may now be considered owners, or the original creator/owner may transfer the rights of copyright to a stated publisher. Copyright is applicable to items published in printed and digital form, as well as audio and video format.

The copyright symbol for printed material is ©. The copyright symbol for sound recordings is a *P* with a circle around it. Copyright is granted for a set period of time. As laws have changed, the set period of time established for copyrighted material has changed. Currently, a term of copyright is equal to the length of the life of the author/creator plus fifty years. For many songs written before 1978, the copyright term is ninety-five years from date of publication. Items created and published before 1923 in the United States are considered to be in the public domain. "Public domain" means the material is no longer protected under copyright law because its legally set period of time has expired.

You do not have to register a copyright in order to own something you create. Under US law, you automatically own the copyright from the moment you create something in tangible form. Many people register for a copyright so that their creation is on file and documented as the copyrighted creation, thereby legalizing their ownership of

Chapter 2: Application of Law to the Life of the Church

that particular idea and providing an obstacle for others who might attempt to copyright the same or very similar things.

Even materials that do not contain a copyright symbol are not necessarily free and available for us to use. Items registered with the US Copyright Office after March 1989 no longer require the copyright symbol.

When something is copyrighted the owner is given exclusive right to determine the following in relation to the work or product:

- ✓ Reproduction
- ✓ Distribution
- ✓ Adaptation
- ✓ Public performance
- ✓ Public display
- ✓ Translations into other languages
- ✓ Translations into other media

Plagiarism is the act of stealing and passing off another's ideas, words, or other intellectual property as one's own original work. As it pertains to our work of ministry, both in the church and beyond the church into the world, there are at least two exceptions to copyright of which we need to be aware. They are:

Fair-Use Exception

Copyrighted material may be used if it is being used in a fair manner that does not take away from the creator/owner in any way. This is often determined by the purpose and character of the use, the nature of the copyrighted work, and the amount and substance of the portion of the material being used. It is important to keep in mind that there is not a specified number of words, lines, or notes that constitute the fair-use exception.

The 1961 *Report of the Register of Copyrights on the General Revision of the U.S. Copyright Law* cites examples of activities that courts have regarded as fair use:

- Quotation of excerpts in a review or criticism for purposes of illustration or comment.

- Quotation of short passages in a scholarly or technical work, for illustration or clarification of the author's observations.

- Use in a parody of some of the content of the work parodied.

- Summary of an address or article, with brief quotations, in a news report.

- Reproduction by a library of a portion of a work to replace part of a damaged copy.

- Reproduction by a teacher or student of a small part of a work to illustrate a lesson.

- Reproduction of a work in legislative or judicial proceedings or reports.
- Incidental and fortuitous reproduction, in a newsreel or broadcast, of a work located at the scene of an event being reported.

Religious Services Exemption

According to section 110(3) of the Copyright Law, the "performance of a nondramatic literary or musical work or of a dramatico-musical work of a religious nature, or display of a work [artwork], in the course of services at a place of worship or other religious assembly," is not an infringement of copyright.

This exemption allows, within the context of worship services, the nondramatic performance of musical works and materials from literary sources as well as dramatic musical works of a religious nature, and the display of artwork. The exemption does not give us permission to reproduce a copyrighted work, distribute the work, display or make copies of lyrics to songs/hymns, make a new arrangement or derivative work of a copyrighted piece of material, make a digital sound or video recording, or transmit the totality of our worship service via the Internet, television, radio, or satellite.

It is also interesting to note that this exemption does not extend to copyrighted material that is offered during business sessions at a religious gathering, or music or dramas that might be offered during banquets, retreats, or youth activities.

I am certain that after reading all this you are wringing your hands, wondering how in the world you are going to be able to engage any digital materials safely, legally, and ethically. You can take a deep breath now! There are many safe, cost-effective, and easy-to-navigate options available to you and your context of ministry. Let us consider these options, even as we explore the scenario presented at the beginning of this chapter.

Photographs, Clip Art, and Images

The church discussed in this scenario does not have a standard picture or image on the front of its worship bulletin. Instead, it scours a variety of different resources to find an image or images that relate well to the topic of the day. The best practice would be to begin with what you already have access to legally and easily. Consider the clip art, images, and pictures included in your computer software. Because you have purchased the software, the images contained within it are for your use without any additional copyright permission. It is also very common for software developers to have a website link available within the software to lead you to more clip art, photos, and so on. A great example of this is Microsoft Office. If you want to insert clip art, you will find a fair amount of options within the computer. There is a link to lead you to a much more expansive library of photos and images available from the Microsoft website. All of these are free and legally available for use.

Consider also the available variety of different subscriptions that provide images to you and your organization. Some subscriptions are a "pay as you use" type of setup, while others may be purchased annually as a group. Some examples of websites offering

Chapter 2: Application of Law to the Life of the Church

online subscriptions that you may be familiar with are Clipart.com, Shutterstock, Fotolia, Textweek, and GraphicStock.

It is also important to recognize and celebrate the local talent that may be among you. Be mindful of those of all ages who have the gift of artistry. You may be surprised at the variety of art expressions available within your congregation to help make your church's time of worship even more full and glorious, if you only ask.

A word of caution: Just because you can access a variety of different images online does not automatically mean that they are free. Some images that appear on the Internet are copyright-protected. Give credit where credit is due. Seek permission or pay the necessary fees to use artwork, whether from the Internet or another source, that is not of your own creation. All of us, clergy and lay leaders in ministry alike, would do well to remember that how we run our ministries is a witness to those around us who are watching as we do our work.

> You may be surprised at the variety of art expressions available within your congregation to help make your church's time of worship even more full and glorious, if you only ask.

Music and Video Licenses

The above scenario tells us that a live band shares in worship leadership at Perfection Church as they perform contemporary music that has been recorded by licensed artists. The lyrics are displayed on screens as a way to encourage participation by the congregation. There is also a variety of video clips incorporated into worship and the teaching life of the community. This type of scenario is occurring more and more in faith communities. As you seek to do the right thing, here are a few points to keep in mind:

- A best practice is to purchase music and video licenses. There are a variety of different licenses that religious and nonprofit organizations can purchase on an annual basis that provide legal permission to use copyrighted music and videos. The licensing agency acts as a clearinghouse for publishers and composers by obtaining copyright permission for you. Churches and some other Christian nonprofit organizations are permitted to make copies of copyrighted music and songs for use in worship, with certain conditions. The license also gives churches permission to make audio and video recordings of services that contain copyrighted music, within certain parameters and specifications.

  There are also options within many of the license packages to stream and transmit copyrighted material that you have permission to use within the course of a religious service of worship. The music performance license will often also give you permission to display (on-screen or in print) the lyrics to the songs you are using. A video license will grant permission to use videos that are otherwise copyrighted for home use only to be used in worship or teaching settings. Some of the more well-known license companies are SongNet, OneLicense, CVLI, and CCLI. ASCAP (American Society of Composers, Authors, and Publishers) and BMI (Broadcast Music, Inc.) are much larger music licensing companies that cater to restaurants, corporate settings, and large public venues. They offer more coverage and a broader scope of music genres than the average faith community would need or could afford.

- Even if you have purchased licenses to use copyrighted music and video, you still must exercise caution. Not everything is covered under the licenses you purchase. Some composers, musicians, and producers prefer not to be covered under a larger license. (The larger, subscription-based licenses provide an exhaustive list of artists, composers, etc. that are covered.) In these cases, it is imperative that you seek permission directly from the company in order to use their material.

YouTube

YouTube is one of the largest online video hosting sites in the world. It is fairly easy to add your videos to YouTube, to share videos you have found on the site that you like, and to copy and reuse in a different setting a video you believe to be relevant in worship or spiritual formation. Please be aware that much of what is on YouTube is copyrighted information that has been posted without appropriate permission. YouTube is not responsible for "policing" legal and illegal information. On October 28, 1998, President Bill Clinton signed the Digital Millennium Copyright Act (DMCA) into law. The DMCA designated Internet service providers (the ISPs that connect consumers to the Internet) and websites (and other online service providers) as "safe harbors." What does it mean to be a "safe harbor"? It means that YouTube is not held responsible when your niece uploads an unauthorized video clip of a *Hannah Montana* TV show, as long as YouTube cooperates with the actual owners of the clip if they ask that it be taken down. This "safe harbor" provision is often taken for granted, but its importance cannot be underestimated; no website could allow users to post videos, pictures, or even words if the website owner were held responsible for the content of each post. In order to keep "safe harbor" status, a website or ISP must not knowingly host or provide access to unauthorized copies of a copyrighted work. In addition, when the real owner of a copyrighted work notifies the ISP or website that it is providing access to infringing content, the website or ISP must quickly remove the content or block access to it.

The Holy Bible, Hymnals, and Books of Worship

Please remember that every book published and bound is protected by copyright. Yes, even the Bible! It is important to note what version of the Bible you are using, especially if you are sharing a specific scripture or text (in a bulletin or on a screen). It is also important to read the copyright permissions and restrictions that are found on the copyright page of every resource you use. Just because it is produced by the church or made for use by the church does not mean there are not boundaries on the ways in which it can be used.

Remember, the careful balancing point that exists even as we try to navigate the world of copyright law, ethical and appropriate behavior, and the multimedia world in which we live is that of respect for one another. How do we honor, value, and respect the work of another while also wanting to share that work with others because of what it provokes within us and offers to us as we seek to be faithful disciples of Jesus Christ? We won't always get it right. What is important is that we try for right, even when right means more work and sometimes more creativity.

Chapter 2: Application of Law to the Life of the Church

Selection, Hiring, and Supervision

First Church is a large congregation located in an affluent suburban area. Reverend Howe, the lead pastor, was served with a lawsuit last week alleging that he, individually, and First Church are liable for injuries suffered by a parishioner of the church. The lawsuit alleges that First Church, as the employer, and Reverend Howe, as the supervisor of an associate pastor, negligently hired and supervised the associate pastor, resulting in the sexual abuse of a parishioner by the associate pastor. Reverend Howe called the church's attorney upon receiving the lawsuit. The church's attorney immediately began to investigate the matter.

Eighteen months ago, First Church leaders decided to expand the clergy staff with the addition of a new associate pastor. The new associate pastor would have extensive responsibilities for counseling and visitation of the sick and homebound members. When the search began, they received dozens of inquiries and applications. The selection committee interviewed several candidates and ultimately offered the job to a young man, Reverend Smyth, who had impressed them in the interview. Reverend Smyth was glib and charismatic, and he seemed to have good references and academic credentials. He was a seminary graduate with chaplaincy experience and had been serving in a congregation of moderate size several hundred miles away. When Reverend Smyth accepted their offer and agreed to start in just two weeks, the selection committee considered its work to be finished. They didn't contact the seminary or any of his work references.

Reverend Smyth started work at First Church and seemed to be making great progress in getting acquainted with the parishioners. His counseling schedule became fairly busy and the church leaders were gratified to see that he was being welcomed and accepted. Within three months of his arrival, Mrs. White had come to see him several times for marital counseling. She described the circumstances of her marriage and her increasing dissatisfaction with her relationship with her husband. Reverend Smyth had been divorced before coming to First Church, and he shared details of his experience with Mrs. White in the course of their first counseling sessions.

In a very short amount of time, Mrs. White began asking Reverend Smyth to meet her for counseling somewhere other than his office at the church. He agreed to her invitation. They met in several places, including her home, a hotel, and a national park campground. Between counseling sessions, they called each other every day, exchanged dozens of text messages and e-mails every day, and made efforts to see each other as often as possible. This went on for more than six months before Reverend Howe noticed anything unusual about the interaction between Reverend Smyth and Mrs. White. Honestly, he might not have noticed then except for the fact that a friend in another church called him and told him to watch out for Mrs. White. Reverend Howe was told that she had "caused trouble" in his friend's church by making allegations of a sexual relationship with one of the pastors.

Reverend Howe called Reverend Smyth into his office and advised him to be careful in all his relationships with parishioners, especially women, and to follow the church's standards in his counseling appointments—including meeting the counselees only in the office, meeting only during usual business hours, and referring counselees to professional therapists if more than three sessions were requested.

Notes

Safe Sanctuaries in a Virtual World

Reverend Smyth assured Reverend Howe that he understood and would certainly follow the protocols.

Reverend Howe was busy with the church's annual financial campaign. He didn't receive any more calls about Mrs. White. Reverend Smyth seemed to be busily involved in a variety of programs and with a variety of people. Then Mr. White called and asked for an appointment.

Mr. White shared that he believed his wife was involved with another man, possibly another member of the church. He didn't know the identity of the man his wife might be involved with. He was distraught and sought advice for repairing his marriage. Reverend Howe offered guidance and prayer. A couple of weeks later, Mr. White called Reverend Howe to thank him for his help and to say that he and Mrs. White were moving to a new community about a hundred miles away. He was being transferred there by his employer.

Mrs. White sent Reverend Smyth dozens of text messages and e-mails with details about the move to a new location. She invited him again and again to come to her new home. With minimal hesitation, Reverend Smyth accepted her invitation, and thus their relationship continued—even though they were miles apart. Over the next couple of months, their text messages to each other became more and more sexualized, and their phone conversations included at least a few minutes of telling each other what sexual behavior they would engage in when they were together again. Nevertheless, Reverend Smyth continued counseling other parishioners at First Church, including several other women. For a few months, he was involved with Mrs. White and also beginning a new relationship with a woman who was a new member of First Church, Ms. Singleton. Finally, Reverend Smyth proposed marriage to Ms. Singleton, and he informed Mrs. White that he would no longer be able to continue to see her for counseling or any other purpose.

This announcement from Reverend Smyth left Mrs. White distraught and fearful. She worried that Reverend Smyth would reveal what had happened between them to his new fiancée or to Mr. White. She worried about what the consequences of such a revelation might be. She decided to confess to her husband what had happened. When Mr. White heard that his wife had indeed been involved with a man at the church—not a parishioner, but the associate pastor—he was outraged. He immediately called Reverend Howe and demanded that Reverend Smyth be discharged for his unethical and immoral conduct. Reverend Howe tried to respond with pastoral reassurances; however, he gave no promise to Mr. White about the continuing employment of Reverend Smyth. Mr. White was left with the impression that Reverend Howe wasn't taking the situation very seriously.

In actuality, Reverend Howe took action that very day. He called Reverend Smyth and the chairman of the personnel committee to a meeting and shared Mr. White's report with both of them. He asked for Reverend Smyth's resignation and Reverend Smyth acquiesced. They demanded the return of the church-owned cell phone and laptop computer. They accompanied him to his office and witnessed his removal of personal possessions there. Finally, they escorted him from the church and instructed him to have no further contact with any parishioners. Reverend Howe hoped this was the end of a very ugly situation.

Chapter 2: Application of Law to the Life of the Church

Negligent Selection

Negligence is defined in one popular publication as "carelessness or a failure to exercise reasonable care."[1] *Merriam-Webster's Collegiate Dictionary*, eleventh edition, defines *negligence* as "failure to exercise the care that a reasonably prudent person would exercise in like circumstances."

For our purposes, let's think of "negligent selection" with the understanding that we are including in this concept the hiring of paid workers as well as the selection of unpaid volunteer workers in the church's ministries. In the context of selection of workers—paid or volunteer—in the church, negligent selection would entail not being reasonably careful in the choice of workers. Allegations of negligent selection and hiring come up when the church's choice of a worker is careless and leads to a foreseeable injury.

A church faces significant liability for injuries caused by its workers. The church is not a guarantor of complete safety for all parishioners or participants in the church's ministries. However, the church must be reasonably prudent in selecting workers to carry out its programs and ministries. The church is responsible, in the consideration of negligence claims, for harm resulting from the church's failure to exercise reasonable care in its operations and ministries.

Negligence in the selection of workers by the church is very often alleged in claims of sexual misconduct, sexual abuse, and child abuse; as well as in claims of the careless operation of a church vehicle and in claims of financial fraud or exploitation.

Failure by the church to be reasonably careful in the selection of workers for ministries, whether involving children, youth, or adults, can lead to very costly settlements or verdicts against the church. Sexual misconduct or unethical behavior by a worker with an adult parishioner, or abuse or harm of a child in any form by a worker, volunteer, or employee, has led in many cases to judgments in the millions of dollars. In a ten-year period, the cost to resolve such claims, not including legal fees, approached $100 million in one denomination. This makes it clear that each claim has the potential to bankrupt your church, both financially and spiritually.

Let's think about the reasons that claims of misconduct are such a huge risk for a church. We sometimes hear participants in classes we teach on this topic say, "Oh, you must be exaggerating. In our church we know everyone. It couldn't happen here." Or, "Nobody would sue our church! We trust each other."

These comments reflect some significant factors. Churches are very trusting communities, and the members generally believe that all who participate in the ministries share a depth of faith and a moral code that would protect them from misconduct and abuse. Churches are usually very open and welcoming organizations with many opportunities for joining in events and programs. Unfortunately, these seemingly good "faith factors" can lead to the church being an easy place for an abuser to find his or her next target or victim.

There are several other factors that make sexual misconduct such a huge risk. In our classes, we sometimes hear participants say, "Well, even if we are sued, our insurance will cover us." Others say, "If we are sued, it won't matter. This church is so poor, we

Notes

Safe Sanctuaries in a Virtual World

couldn't pay a judgment anyway." At this point in each class session, we try to clarify the issues such comments point to. Insurance coverage for claims of misconduct or sexual abuse is very limited, if not excluded entirely. The leaders of the church must review the insurance policy in effect carefully to know exactly how much, if any, coverage there is for such claims. Even if the congregation doesn't have thousands of dollars in its bank account, it has valuable property—the land and buildings—that could be lost in the event of a judgment against the church.

Finally, it is important to understand that sexual misconduct lawsuits and child abuse lawsuits almost always include allegations that the harm suffered by the victim was a direct or proximate result of the church's negligent selection of the alleged perpetrator of the abuse as an employee or volunteer. Therefore, all of these factors illustrate that it is crucial for your church to be very aware of the need for strong selection procedures when choosing staff workers and volunteers.

> Today, our churches can and should consider the social media presence of each staff member, and potential staff member, as part of our selection processes.

Today, our churches can and should consider the social media presence of each staff member, and potential staff member, as part of our selection processes. Twenty-five years ago, when lawsuits against churches for negligent selection of clergy and clergy sexual misconduct began coming to our attention, the standard selection process would not have included asking a candidate for a review of his or her social media accounts or pages! Today, every personnel committee or board of ordination needs to include this in the application and ordination processes. Why? We need to use this tool because the individuals seeking positions in the church have online virtual presences that reflect their beliefs, values, and typical behavior, all of which contain information for consideration in the selection process. In addition, online media are being used more and more frequently by individuals to express their emotions and opinions regarding everything from the weather to their former employers.

The church can and should adopt and use policies regarding the use of social media by its workers.

Best Practices to Reduce Liability for Negligent Selection Claims

Organize your church's selection procedures for workers, paid and volunteer, with these specific processes:

Written applications: Ask each candidate for the position to complete a written application form. This will provide you with basic information, including the person's address, employment history (and volunteer history), education and experience, and references, including contact information. Use this as the initial basis for your consideration of each applicant. Include on the application form an authorization from the applicant that allows the reference contacts to speak truthfully with you without fear of reprisal from the applicant. What is the cost to use this selection tool? Your costs will be the cost of the paper and the time it takes to process the information gathered on the application. What is the value of using this selection tool? You'll acquire a substantial record of information pertinent to the candidate and his or her qualifications and experience relative to the position.

Chapter 2: Application of Law to the Life of the Church

References: Ask the applicant to provide two or three references—both employment and personal. You may also ask for a reference from the applicant's previous or current church/congregation. Follow through with verifying and communicating with each reference given. Keep a record of the comments made by each person giving a reference. What is the cost for using this selection tool? The time it takes to contact and talk with each reference. What is the value of using this selection tool? You may gain information from the references that will be very helpful in your evaluation and selection process. Persons who are giving references may be more willing to give you the information simply because they want to be cooperative with the church.

Criminal background check: Include a separate Fair Credit Reporting Act–compliant written disclosure and authorization for completion of a criminal background check and other background checks for each application. As indicated above, the scope of the authorization should include not only prior to employment of the individual but also throughout his or her service to your organization. For any applicant being seriously considered, the background checks are an important selection tool, as well as an important tool for ongoing evaluation. The criminal background check can be used to check the applicant's driving record as well as to reveal any criminal convictions in your local jurisdiction, nationally and internationally. However, many perpetrators of child abuse, for example, have not been convicted of any crime, and thus a criminal background check will not reveal a criminal record. Nevertheless, using this as a selection tool is important for the church. By adding other types of screening, an organization can improve the depth of understanding they gain about the individual. For example, a record of multiple risk-related behaviors will often be revealed in the course of conducting the check (a check of a driver's license may reveal multiple traffic fines related to high speeds, and running stop signs; a civil record check may reveal a high number of civil actions in which the individual has been involved; a résumé verification may reveal employers not listed; an address history may reveal addresses not revealed by the candidate). In the event of a lawsuit alleging negligent selection of a worker, the church's record of conducting a comprehensive background check will be helpful in demonstrating that the church was reasonably prudent in its selection of the alleged abuser. What is the cost of using criminal background screening as a selection tool? Your church can have a complete and thorough background screen prepared for each applicant. The fees can range from nine to ninety-five dollars, depending on how comprehensive the search and the types of records (identity verification, criminal, civil, driving, credit, reference, substance testing, address history, résumé verification, education verification, and employment history, for example) being examined. There is also a time cost for preparing and reviewing the background checks, which is minimal in comparison to the protection it will afford the church in the event of a negligent selection lawsuit. What is the value of using criminal background screening? As mentioned above, standard use of these forms can be valuable in showing that the church was reasonably prudent in its selection of each worker.

Personal interviews: A personal interview is a necessary selection tool. Many churches and businesses today conduct telephone interviews (or use Skype or another similar method), rather than in-person interviews in the first stage of a search to fill a position. Especially when the church receives a high number of applications, such a method may be helpful in reducing the number to whom you will give serious consideration.

> The church can and should adopt and use policies regarding the use of social media by its workers.

Safe Sanctuaries in a Virtual World

When you reduce the list to several top candidates, it's time to schedule the in-person interviews. What is the cost of using the personal interview as a primary selection tool? The time spent in preparing for and conducting the interview will be perhaps the biggest cost. What is the value of the personal interview? No other selection tool will provide you with an equivalent opportunity to evaluate and understand the applicant's skills, talents, experience, and qualifications for the position to be filled. It is important to train your selection committee on behavioral interviews and/or to include someone on the committee who has knowledge and experience in this area. How a candidate sits, speaks, and responds to questions will reveal much about what is occurring behind the scenes for that individual. Training in these skills is a prerequisite, as many of our natural instincts about people will and can mislead us into trusting someone who reveals behaviorally that he or she is not trustworthy. Other selection methods might provide information, but in the personal interview you will be able to see for yourselves (you and the selection committee) whether the information you have gathered really matches the presentation of the individual candidate.

Six-month hospitality rule for volunteers/Conditional offer of employment for paid workers: In the selection of volunteer leaders in the church's ministries, the six-month hospitality rule sets a protocol by which new persons aren't placed in leadership during the first six months of their membership. During the six-month period, the new members who are potential volunteers have an opportunity to experience the variety of the church's ministries, and the church leaders have opportunities to interact with the new members and observe the members' gifts and graces for ministry leadership. What is the cost of using the six-month hospitality rule as a selection tool? The church won't be able to immediately place new members, and this may seem to create a temporary scarcity of volunteers. However, the value of this selection tool is that it prevents unqualified persons from having immediate opportunity or access to vulnerable persons. Using the six-month hospitality rule as a standard part of your church's selection process will be helpful if the church needs to demonstrate that it was reasonably prudent in its selection and placement of persons in ministries.

The six-month hospitality rule can also be used, with some modification, in the selection of paid workers. It would generally be impractical to offer employment to an individual and at the same time prohibit that person from working. However, by using a conditional offer of employment, the church can allow the candidate to begin work with the understanding that a final offer of employment is conditional upon satisfactory completion of a probationary period of three to six months. This can afford both the church and the newly hired employee a period of observation and acclimation similar to the six-month hospitality rule for volunteers.

Review of the candidate's online presence in social media: This is a relatively new selection tool available to employers or churches regarding candidates for employed or volunteer positions. Many churches haven't begun to include this in their selection process even if they have developed standard policies for the use of electronic communication technologies and social media in ministry. For purposes of promoting best practices in the operation of the church's ministries, we believe review of a candidate's online presence in social media is important. Recently, I saw a television ad promoting an online application that will organize and gather into one online address all of my online identities and the social media I'm using. The popularity of this product is

Chapter 2: Application of Law to the Life of the Church

evidence that many individuals have created multiple online, or virtual, identities and might like assistance with keeping the identities organized!

As the church evaluates each candidate for leadership, it is valuable to know how the applicant presents himself or herself in the virtual world. Asking the applicant to share personal online media postings as part of the selection process, not surreptitiously looking for online information, is the recommended process. The church has the freedom to select only those candidates who share its values and beliefs, and this can be determined through the personal impressions gained from interviews as well as from references and what is found online. Just as the church would be careful to evaluate reference information for reliability, so it also needs to be careful in its evaluation of what is found online. In the event that unacceptable postings are found during the selection process, the church and the candidate have a chance to discuss the findings. The church also has another opportunity to share its standards for online communication. The candidate has an opportunity to decide whether or not to conform to the church's standards and continue in the selection process. What would be the cost to the church of including a review of the online presence of candidates as a selection tool? The biggest cost will be the time it takes to have the conversation with the candidates and the time it takes to look over the online postings. What would be the value to the church? Using this tool during the selection process will help guide the church in its choices as well as guide the candidate in his or her understanding of what will be expected if an offer of employment or volunteer placement is made.

Use of these selection procedures will support your church's development of a strong hiring and selection policy and protocol and thus your church's development of an excellent staff of paid and volunteer workers.

Your church's personnel committee is likely composed of volunteers who serve one or two years. This means that you will have a recurring need for training the new members of the committee. Training about the specific selection procedures and the value of each one needs to be provided annually, or whenever new members are added.

Putting the Information into Context

Let's consider the hypothetical situation at First Church given on pages 27–28. Take some time individually, and then as a small group, to consider your responses to the following questions:

- *When First Church began its search for a new associate pastor, how did they proceed? What avenues did they pursue to identify candidates for the position?*
- *When the committee decided which applicants to interview, how did they proceed? What steps did they use to learn about Reverend Smyth's qualifications?*
- *In light of the lawsuit that was filed, and its allegations, what could First Church have done in its search-and-selection process to make a more well-informed decision in its selection of the new associate pastor?*
- *What would have been the value of checking Reverend Smyth's references? What would have been the value of checking his academic record at the seminary?*

Safe Sanctuaries in a Virtual World

Negligent Supervision and Retention of Workers

Let's remember *Merriam-Webster's* definition of *negligence*: "failure to exercise the care that a reasonably prudent person would exercise in like circumstances." In the previous sections we studied negligence with respect to selecting church workers, both paid and volunteer staff members. Negligent selection allegations arise in situations where it appears the church may not have been reasonably careful in choosing one or more of its workers, and someone was injured as a result.

In this section, we will focus on a somewhat different type of negligence: the negligent retention of workers. You may recall from the hypothetical case that the lead pastor, Reverend Howe, received a phone call from a friend in another church. He was told to watch out because Mrs. White had "caused trouble" in the friend's church. Reverend Howe didn't know at the time of this phone call that Reverend Smyth and Mrs. White had already begun a counseling relationship that quickly became inappropriate. He didn't know that Reverend Smyth had begun meeting her at places away from the church. Nevertheless, he had a conversation with Reverend Smyth and advised him that in counseling parishioners he must follow the church's standard procedures, including meeting only at the church office, meeting during normally scheduled business hours, meeting for no more than three sessions, and making referrals to another counselor if the parishioner requested more than three sessions. Reverend Smyth said he agreed with the church's standards and assured Reverend Howe that he would uphold the standards in his counseling.

Reverend Howe was saddened when he met with Mr. White and learned that he suspected his wife was involved with another man who was possibly a parishioner. He offered his guidance and prayers for Mr. White. However, he didn't share the information with Reverend Smyth, and he didn't suspect that Reverend Smyth might actually be the one involved inappropriately with Mrs. White. When Mr. White called to let Reverend Howe know about his job transfer, Reverend Howe offered words of encouragement.

After Mr. and Mrs. White moved out of the community, however, Reverend Howe did fail to notice several things that might have been important. He was responsible for supervising the work of Reverend Smyth. He didn't pay attention to Reverend Smyth's usual work schedule or the dates, times, and locations of his counseling appointments. He didn't schedule regular conversations with Reverend Smyth to review his work and his responsibilities. He didn't routinely ask Reverend Smyth to turn in expense reports. He didn't review the Internet usage or cell phone bills for the church's cell phones and computers that were being used by Reverend Smyth as well as other staff members. He didn't check in with parishioners to ask for their perceptions of Reverend Smyth and what they felt his gifts and graces for ministry might be. The personnel committee didn't ask either Reverend Howe or Reverend Smyth for periodic reports, and the committee didn't meet with either of the ministers on a regular basis.

When Reverend Howe received the phone call from Mr. White informing him of the relationship between Reverend Smyth and Mrs. White, Reverend Howe was surprised, to say the least. Later, he was shocked when he received the lawsuit containing allegations that he and the church had been negligent in the supervision of Reverend

Chapter 2: Application of Law to the Life of the Church

Smyth. He wondered what he could have done to be more diligent in supervising Reverend Smyth, as well as the other staff members. He asked the church's attorney, "How can we be accused of negligent supervision when we never received any complaints about him?"

Generally, attorneys teach their clients that negligent supervision claims may arise when a worker is retained after the employer has received some information that indicates the specific worker may pose a risk of harm to others. Negligent-supervision allegations frequently are made in cases of sexual misconduct, child abuse, playground injuries, and sometimes automobile accidents on retreats or other trips.

In a case of child abuse, the victim's parent may believe the injury wouldn't have happened if the church staff member—such as a preschool teacher or a youth group leader—had been adequately supervised in his or her work. Consider this example: A church hired a youth director using thorough screening procedures, including criminal background checks and interviews. The youth director began working, and the lead pastor provided him with orientation training as well as close supervision for the first few months. As the months passed, the lead pastor became less involved with direct supervision, and he stopped attending youth group meetings. The lead pastor was very surprised when he received a call from the youth director asking him to come to the police station and post bond. The charge was sexual assault of a minor. The victim was a member of the youth group. The victim's parents were the ones who made the first report to the police. Then the victim's parents contacted a lawyer to file suit against the church for negligent supervision of the youth director, alleging that the lead pastor's failure to directly observe and supervise the youth director led to the assault suffered by their daughter.

In the case of physical injury, such as on a playground, the victim's parents may believe the injury wouldn't have happened if the preschool director had been supervising the teachers on playground duty.

Let's examine how a claim of negligent supervision might have been made in our First Church hypothetical scenario. Reverend Howe was Reverend Smyth's direct supervisor. Both of them were supervised by the church personnel committee, and the personnel committee was expected to conduct periodic evaluations and reviews of each minister's work performance. The personnel committee usually asked each minister to fill out a report describing his responsibilities and activities, how much time was spent in each area of responsibility, how many parishioners were involved in these activities, and what the minister felt were his most effective activities.

Although the church had been careful in its selection procedures, the diligence seemed to have diminished as soon as Reverend Smyth began to work.

What leads to careless or even negligent supervision in the church and its ministries? In our experience, careless supervision results from several factors:

- The church is a relatively trusting organization/community where the usual assumption is that ministers and staff leaders are individuals who share the faith and moral values of the congregation. The following assumption is that the ministers and staff leaders would not violate the congregation's shared faith and moral values.

Notes

> The costs to the victims of negligent supervision can be life-changing. There is perhaps no real way to calculate the cost when one child is abused in the name of God, or faith, or love.

- The church leaders expect the staff and ministers to be highly qualified and highly committed to the mission and ministry of the church, rather than being committed to their individual best interests.
- The church might not have developed and adopted supervision policies and procedures for the settings of ministry.
- The church might not have provided any orientation or training to its ministers and staff leaders regarding acceptable and unacceptable behaviors.
- The church might not have conducted a thorough evaluation of what character traits, natural talents, behaviors, skills, training, and experience are required.

Review the First Church hypothetical scenario and list the factors you can identify that might indicate negligent supervision of Reverend Smyth:

1.

2.

Consequences of Negligent Supervision: The costs that arise when supervision is inadequate can be huge. In the event of a broken leg suffered on the playground, perhaps the only costs will be those incurred in the victim's medical treatment and care. On the other end of the spectrum, the costs for sexual abuse resulting from allegedly negligent supervision of a paid worker or volunteer can be devastating to the church, ranging from hundreds of thousands to millions of dollars. Beyond the direct financial costs of negligent-supervision cases, there are also more indirect costs, such as damage to the church's reputation in the community and region. When the church's reputation is impugned, a loss of membership, and a decline in new prospects for membership, can have a serious effect on the congregation. When it becomes public knowledge that someone was injured, or nearly injured, because the leaders failed to adequately supervise the ministry, the financial health of the church can be endangered by reduced giving as well as through the payment of a settlement or judgment.

The costs to the victims of negligent supervision can be life-changing. There is perhaps no real way to calculate the cost when one child is abused in the name of God, or faith, or love. If such costs are incalculable, then it might also be true that such costs can never be fully compensated by the church. However, the church must ask, What would it have cost for us to be diligent in our supervision of staff and of ministry? The answer is that it would have cost only some time on the part of church leaders. Going forward, the church will always know that this investment of time is what stands between it and bankruptcy—spiritual bankruptcy and financial bankruptcy.

Consequences of Negligent Retention: Let's go back to our hypothetical scenario once again to evaluate the possible claim of negligent retention of Reverend Smyth as the associate pastor of the church. According to the scenario, Reverend Howe had not received any information that indicated any impropriety on the part of Reverend Smyth. Instead, he had heard that Mrs. White had caused trouble in a previous congregation. He heard from Mr. White that their marriage was troubled and he suspected his wife of having an affair. Reverend Howe was not told by anyone that Reverend Smyth and Mrs. White were involved in any type of inappropriate

Chapter 2: Application of Law to the Life of the Church

relationship. Thus, although Reverend Howe had received some information regarding Mrs. White, it doesn't appear that the information gave him any reason to think Reverend Smyth might be involved in misconduct. Reverend Howe did, in fact, as the supervisor, share with Reverend Smyth that he should certainly be careful to follow the church's best practices in counseling Mrs. White.

The hypothetical case continues with describing Reverend Howe's focus on the church's fund-raising and his lack of attention to the day-to-day work habits and presence of Reverend Smyth. Honestly, neither Reverend Howe nor the personnel committee conducted even an informal conversation with Reverend Smyth to find out how his work and ministry were progressing or what areas he felt he needed assistance with. Perhaps the committee's lack of review with Reverend Smyth on a periodic basis could be characterized as negligent supervision.

Although the lawsuit brought on behalf of Mr. White alleged that the church negligently retained Reverend Smyth after they knew, or should have known, that Reverend Smyth was engaging in misconduct, the facts described above (and in the complete hypothetical scenario) would not likely support such allegations. The church did not retain the perpetrator of misconduct after being informed of his misconduct. Furthermore, the church leaders escorted him off the property and instructed him to have no additional contact with the parishioners. Even though Mr. White might have appreciated being informed that Reverend Howe had terminated the employment of Reverend Smyth, no one at the church was obligated to provide that information to him.

There is another element to consider. If Reverend Howe had called Mr. White, or gone to visit him personally, and shared with him that Reverend Smyth was no longer employed at the church as a result of what Mr. White had reported, what might have been the result? Do you think Reverend Howe could have offered any emotional support for Mr. White, or any spiritual guidance? If so, might that have defused Mr. White's anger and led him not to file suit against the church?

Many attorneys would not encourage the church to consider the idea, in a situation such as this, that the church must always be the church—the source of healing and grace—even though delivering healing and grace could be very painful for the church. A number of attorneys hold a different view. Specifically, we hope the church, through its leaders, will make all possible efforts to set right the harmful situations where abuse is found in its community. We believe the reward will be ministry protection in its fullest measure.

Best Practices for Minimizing Negligent Supervision Liability

Our focus here is minimizing the likelihood of negligent supervision in ministry, especially as we think about ministry in the virtual world. First let's look at the list of recommended operating procedures for ministry we usually think of as taking place "in person" or "face-to-face" between individuals. Then we will apply those best practices to our online ministries.

Two adult leaders in every setting: This best practice is intended to ensure that in case of emergency, there will be at least one leader who can call for help and one who can, for example, give first aid. It is also intended to reduce the possibility that one leader could isolate a victim in secrecy and cause harm or injury without being discovered. In some situations, of course, two leaders are not enough. You simply must staff the ministry with adequate numbers of adult leaders for the number of participants. The adequate number can be larger than two, but it is unlikely to be less than two. The hypothetical situation we studied at the beginning of this section specifically involved misconduct that began in a pastoral counseling setting. The context of pastoral counseling is a special case, and we will more fully examine it in subsequent pages.

No leader under the age of eighteen, and leaders should be more than five years older than those they are responsible for: A common example for this best practice is that of senior high youth group leaders. It is easy to understand that putting a nineteen-year-old college student into the role of leader of a group of sixteen- to eighteen-year-olds might create unwise situations.

A window in each door or an open door: This best practice calls for all staff members, whether laypersons or clergy, to have an open-door policy (meaning that a door is literally left open, not just that all have freedom to enter the room) at the office, or to have an uncovered window in a closed door. Failure to follow this operating procedure too easily creates opportunities for isolation of a staff person with a victim.

Name tags, identification badges, or uniforms: This best practice calls for all staff members to have name tags or identification badges that must be worn or displayed when at work. More importantly, badges should identify the scope of authorization granted and the clearance level given to an individual. For example, volunteer badges should specify "Child care Volunteer," "General Greeter Volunteer," "Financial Support Volunteer," "Administrative Support Volunteer," "Pastoral Services Volunteer," and the like. Clearances should not be granted until all background checks are completed.

Check-in and check-out procedures for events: This best practice, in some form, is often used in children's ministry and youth ministry. It is also common in ministry with older adults. It is very valuable in reducing the likelihood that a participant could be isolated and targeted by a perpetrator of abuse during an event or removed from the event by an unauthorized individual.

Training for each leadership position and event: This best practice provides training to all the leaders for specific events and ministries. Training may need to include first aid, teaching methods, and how to recognize the indicators of abuse in children or older adults, as well as proper use of technology and communication tools.

Reporting abuse or suspected abuse according to your state's laws: This best practice includes knowing what your state's law requires and understanding how to comply with those requirements. Church leaders must review the law each year and train all clergy and lay workers thoroughly. Failure to follow your state's laws in reporting abuse not only can lead to the injury of vulnerable individuals but can also lead to claims of negligent supervision.

Chapter 2: Application of Law to the Life of the Church

Permissions: This best practice includes having a signed permission form on record for each participant in the ministry that is up-to-date and specific to the context or event.

Evaluation of staff leaders: This best practice includes regular observation of the work of church staff leaders, both clergy and volunteers. This practice also includes periodic formal review and evaluation of the work of church leaders to ensure that each one is following the policies and procedures the church has adopted as its best practices. In the event any leader is found not to be following the church's best practices, a review will provide the opportunity for correction and redirection if needed.

Even in the simplest of ministries, utilizing these operating procedures as the church's best practices can build a strong framework of ministry protection for all leaders and participants.

At first glance, these best practices might not seem to be applicable to our protocols and procedures for ministry communications and technology use. Look again. Taken as a whole, these best practices are designed to prevent isolation and secrecy, and our communications must also be designed to prevent isolation and secrecy. *Confidentiality* and *secrecy* are not synonymous. In ministry, confidentiality is very important, but when confidentiality is used inappropriately, it can be very harmful.

Maintaining appropriate communication channels and tools in the ministry of the church must be given a high priority in the church's planning for ministry protection. Now let's apply the operating procedure guidelines given above to online communications.

Two adult leaders: For communication policies, this translates to making your online/e-mail/social media messages open to review by more than one person. For example, in youth ministry, the communication policy should be that when e-mail or text messages are sent, the messages go to the group, and parents are included in the group. This type of procedure ensures that multiple people have knowledge of how and when the church is communicating with its membership. One option available to churches is computer-monitoring software and restriction on websites that can be accessed through those computers.

No leader under the age of eighteen, and leaders should be more than five years older than those they are responsible for: The church cannot realistically control the use of communication tools such as e-mail or social media by children and youth who have access to their own phones and computers. Persons involved in your ministries will inevitably use their personal devices to get messages out. However, the church can be sure that the leaders responsible for communication regarding the ministries and who are using the church's technology are adults who are following the church's procedures. Youth who are involved in volunteer leadership roles can be given thorough training in the acceptable uses of the church's communication tools and online resources.

A window in each door or an open door: In a communications context, this best practice means that staff members are aware that their use of communication tools is not private or secret.

Notes

Safe Sanctuaries in a Virtual World

Name tags, identification badges, or uniforms: In the context of social media communication, this best practice refers to the church's use of online user names, passwords, and other identifiers. Your church, for ministry protection, must develop a policy for sending, receiving, reviewing, and storing or removing messages such as e-mails, texts, social media postings, and online photos. Decide who will have access to passwords, how often the identifiers and passwords must be changed, and where those records will be maintained. Then, on a regular basis, train all the staff and leaders in your church's policies and practices.

Check-in and check-out procedures for events: Some organizations are using online check-in and check-out for certain events, as well as online signature of permissions or waivers. (Many churches are even using online methods for payment of parishioners' tithes and offerings.) Each of these uses of technology must, for ministry protection, be carefully designed and implemented. All staff members with responsibilities in these areas must be fully trained in the safe use of each program, and periodic updates should be provided. If your church is using these types of communication tools, be sure that you work with highly experienced, qualified, and knowledgeable leaders to implement the plans. Don't leave anything to chance, and don't assume that no one would try to take advantage of the church through inappropriate, even criminal, use of the technology. That level of misplaced trust and denial will inevitably lead to failures of ministry protection and loss of a church's integrity.

Training for each leadership position and event: Every time your church creates a new social media avenue or implements a new use of communications technology, include appropriate training for all the staff and leaders. Be sure that everyone who will use the program actually understands how it operates, what it is used for, and who will have access to it. Every new staff person and volunteer leader needs to be trained as they begin their work.

Permissions: Include in the church's best communications practices a policy that requires permission from parents and guardians for electronic or online communication between children or youth and staff or church leaders. Include in your standard practices a policy that prevents individuals from being named in the church's online and electronic images.

Evaluation of staff leaders: In general, we find that churches are not requiring a periodic review of staff members' work communication skills and practices. For ministry protection, churches need to routinely review the staff members' online or electronic communications to assure proper usage. It is not recommended that such reviews be conducted without the knowledge of the staff members. It is common for churches to expect the lay employees, and especially the clergy, to respond to e-mails, texts, and phone calls immediately upon receipt of the message. The church provides the staff members with cell phones or computers for this purpose. If this is part of your church's operations, it is important to understand that in the event of a claim of negligent supervision of a staff member who is accused of abuse, evidence of the church's failure to periodically review staff communications and uses of church equipment could strengthen the claim of negligence. As your church prepares its best practices for evaluation of staff members, it is very important to recognize that inclusion of communications reviews requires only a small investment of time but may prevent huge losses for the ministry.

Chapter 2: Application of Law to the Life of the Church

BYOD Policies

A number of organizations have begun adopting BYOD (bring your own device) policies instead of supplying employees with company phones or computers, in an effort to avoid the costs of supplying these devices and also to avoid liability for the employee's misuse or abuse of the devices. The BYOD approach is not a complete solution for ministry protection in the church. Your church would be prudent to explore the advantages and disadvantages of this type of policy with an expert in this area before making final decisions on best practices.

Special Case: Pastoral Counseling Operating Procedures

The First Church hypothetical scenario included elements of the ministers' work in the realm of pastoral counseling. Both Reverend Howe and Reverend Smyth were shown to be involved in counseling ministries. The scenario also outlines the church's best practices related to counseling ministries. Many of the ministers you know have responsibility for counseling from time to time. Unfortunately, many churches haven't actually developed a set of standard counseling best practices. In the hypothetical scenario, Reverend Howe articulated that church's counseling best practices. He and church leaders worked to uphold those standards. In addition to the standards described earlier, there are several other best practices that your church can consider as it works to build integrity and protection into your counseling ministries:

Referral to another counselor: If you are not licensed or credentialed as a family counselor, therapist, addiction counselor, pastoral counselor, or any other specific type of counselor, then follow the policy of telling each parishioner who seeks you out for counseling that you are able to offer spiritual guidance but not therapy. If you have specific types of counseling credentials, such as addiction counseling or marriage counseling, then accept only those counselees who are seeking your expertise in these areas. Make it clear that you do not meet individuals or couples more than three times for counseling about a problem for which you aren't qualified to advise, and if additional appointments are desired, you will refer the counselee to another counselor. In the hypothetical scenario, Reverend Smyth failed to uphold this practice, and adverse consequences followed.

No counseling appointments off church property: This best practice is to meet counselees at the church for counseling during regularly scheduled church office hours rather than in some other location or at an unusual time. At the church you are better able to protect confidentiality without promoting secrecy. In a public place you cannot assure that others will not overhear conversation that the counselee would prefer be kept confidential. Also, in an open-door church counseling situation, you are more likely to have the advantage of other individuals being present who understand and might corroborate your appropriate behavior. Reverend Smyth failed to uphold this best practice, and even though he would argue that he was having a personal relationship, not a counseling relationship, the result of his failure to uphold this practice was serious for the church and the individuals involved.

Confidentiality, never secrecy: Each state has a law regarding the requirements for reporting abuse of children, youth, and older or vulnerable adults. These laws always articulate what information can be maintained as confidential. Beyond this, each church or denomination has standards regarding the definition of confidential information and relationships. These two types of requirements—state and church—must be thoroughly understood for the ministers in your church to successfully and safely carry out counseling ministries. Many churches have set a standard practice of informing each new counselee in the first session of the counselor's obligation to report child abuse to law enforcement authorities. This is a reasonable and prudent practice. It shows that the church intends to meet the requirements of the state law and gives the counselee adequate notice to decide what, or how much, information to share in counseling.

Third-person presence rule: Some churches are applying the two-adult rule in situations of pastoral counseling in an effort to minimize the risk of false allegations of abuse or misconduct by a counselor. For example, if the counselee is a female and the pastor is a male, the third person in attendance would preferably be a female. If your church chooses this as a standard practice, it would be wise to inform the counselee at the very beginning of the first session and offer the counselee the opportunity to accept this standard or to decline. In the event the counselee chooses to participate in counseling with the minister and a third person (another minister or counselor), then all three persons may agree in writing that the sessions will be considered private and no one will be authorized to release any information shared in the session. Laws regarding counseling confidentiality and priest-penitent confidentiality should be reviewed by church leaders for a clear understanding of the effects of having a third person present in the counseling session. In the hypothetical scenario we've discussed, the church would have benefited from the use of this practice.

Recording of counseling sessions: Many churches routinely use video recording in their classrooms and preschools. Some churches are beginning to also use video recording in the offices of the church as a protection against false allegations of misconduct. When adopting this as a standard practice, your church leaders will need to plan for regular review of the recordings by at least two persons, preparation of a written report noting any inappropriate behavior observed, and retention of the recordings until the written reports are completed, or indefinite retention. Consultation with experts on these issues would be worthwhile for church leaders. Many ministers we know would be reluctant to use video recording of their counseling appointments, even when the church is already recording classroom sessions. Nevertheless, your church might well decide to give serious consideration to implementing this procedure. In the hypothetical scenario here, recording the counseling appointments of Reverend Smyth might have revealed problematic behavior early on and prevented subsequent difficulty.

Counseling ministries are considered valuable by churches and by individuals. In today's world of communication methods and media, counseling sessions can also be sources of misconduct or false allegations. Develop thoughtfully comprehensive best operating practices to strengthen your church's ability to protect its counseling ministry. The cost for developing these best practices is the time devoted by church leaders initially and then for periodic updates. The benefits will be incalculable!

Chapter 3

Basic Procedures for Ministry in a Virtual World

> But [God has] already made it plain how to live, what to do, what GOD is looking for in men and women. It's quite simple: Do what is fair and just to your neighbor, be compassionate and loyal in your love.
> —Micah 6:8 (THE MESSAGE)

A Story of Power, Pain, and Technology

Grace Church has a thriving youth ministry that involves about seven hundred youth on a weekly basis. Reverend Jones has been serving as the youth minister for six years and is highly regarded by the youth and adults in the church. He is married, and his wife is pregnant with their third child. The programs provided in youth ministry are Sunday school, youth fellowship, weekday Bible study, mission trips to local and international sites, contemporary worship services on Sunday mornings, camping trips, weekend retreats, confirmation studies, youth choir, and youth drama productions. Reverend Jones supervises four youth ministry staff members and a group of at least fifty adult volunteers who participate in the programs on a weekly basis. He takes pride in always being "available" to the youth, their parents, the staff, and the volunteers, and he encourages them to call or text him on his cell phone anytime. He freely shares his cell phone number and e-mail address, and he "friends" all the youth on Facebook.

When school started in September of last year, he invited Sally to become a student leader of the weekday Bible study. She was starting her senior year in high school even though she was only sixteen. Reverend Jones promised her that he would provide all the study material and resources for the weekly sessions and that he would always be at the meetings. He told her it was important for the weekday Bible study to have youth leaders as well as an adult leader. He also told her that participating as a student leader in this program would "look good" on her college applications and that he would give her a strong recommendation. Sally agreed to become a student leader for the weekday Bible study. She enjoyed the preparation meetings with Reverend Jones and the other leaders, and she enjoyed the Bible study sessions. When she eventually asked Reverend Jones to write a recommendation letter for her to the college

Safe Sanctuaries in a Virtual World

she hoped to attend, he did and gave her glowing praise. Sally was thrilled when the college offered her admission and a substantial scholarship.

A few weeks after graduation, Sally attended freshman orientation at the college. On the first evening, she got a call from Reverend Jones on her cell phone. He said he just wanted to tell her how happy he was for her and that he was going to have a hard time finding another student leader for the weekday Bible study who would be as effective as she had been. Orientation lasted four days, and each night Reverend Jones called Sally again. Each time he said he only wanted to be sure she was having a good experience.

In mid-August, Sally left home for her first year of college. Her parents set up her cell phone account on a plan that limited the number of text messages she could send each month; they explained that they wanted her to spend her time studying, not texting. For the first couple of months, Sally's cell phone usage didn't exceed the limits of the plan. Then her mother began to notice that the minutes used were creeping higher and higher. She cautioned Sally to pay attention to her phone usage and not go over the limits. When Sally came home for the Thanksgiving holiday, her father noticed that she seemed worried and anxious, but he thought she was just thinking about her first college exams coming up.

Three weeks later, on the day she was coming home for Christmas, the next phone bill came to Sally's parents. They were astounded to find that Sally had received nearly a thousand text messages, all from the same phone number. The texts were sent to Sally at all hours of the night and day, and on some dates, there were more than a hundred messages. Sally's parents met her at the door with the phone bill in hand. When she saw the phone bill, Sally collapsed in tears.

Sally told her parents that it was Reverend Jones who had been sending all the texts. She told them that it had started with his phone calls each night when she attended orientation. She had asked him not to call her, but he continued to call and also began to text her incessantly. When he wasn't texting her, he was sending e-mails to her college e-mail address or private messaging her on Facebook. He told her that his marriage was in trouble, that he thought he was in love with Sally, and that he dreamed of her running away with him to a new life. Sally told her parents that she didn't know what to do and that she couldn't cope with this anymore. While she was telling her parents what had been going on, her cell phone buzzed with a new incoming text message. It was from Reverend Jones, and it said, "I'm so glad you're back. Meet me in the church parking lot in an hour. I have to see you. I have to touch you. Don't make me wait."

Sally's mother called the police. The detective listened to her story and then went to the church parking lot. Reverend Jones was there, sitting in his car, waiting for Sally. He was arrested for stalking a minor. After more investigation, additional charges of "sexting" a minor were added.

Sally's father called Reverend Thomas, the senior pastor of the church. Reverend Thomas, was shocked, but he believed Sally's father, especially because he had been called last year by another girl's parent with a similar complaint. That family hadn't called the police, and they had agreed to let Reverend Thomas counsel Reverend

Chapter 3: Basic Procedures for Ministry in a Virtual World

Jones to change his behavior. Now, it was clear to Reverend Thomas that it was too late for additional counseling. Reverend Thomas called a meeting of the church's personnel committee and asked for the termination of Reverend Jones's employment at the church. The committee agreed. The resolution of the criminal charges against Reverend Jones will take months.

Consider the following in regard to the above scenario:

- *What can a church do to reduce the likelihood of current or future staff members engaging in such inappropriate behavior with youth?*
- *What can a church do to educate and equip youth and parents to protect themselves from this type of harassing behavior?*
- *What can Grace Church, and the senior pastor, do to restore the trust of Sally, her parents, the parents and youth who first reported the misconduct, and the numbers of people who were shocked to hear of Reverend Jones's behavior?*

The variety of options available to us to engage in digital media, to stay in contact and connection with one another, and to experience the world around us in real or near real time has quickly risen in number in the last fifteen-plus years. The size of computers continues to shrink—from an entire room necessary for the mainframe of a computer to easy-to-handle desktops, laptops, tablets, and cell phones. Mobile phones have progressed from large phones in bags that were tethered to a vehicle for only emergency phone calls, to smaller phones that began to have dual usage as a camera, to today's smart phones that serve as small handheld computers. The Internet has opened us up to worldwide possibilities for gaining and sharing information, accessing television programs and radio shows, and connecting with those who share similar interests, passions, and desires.

Technology is becoming more and more integrated into our everyday lives. Even as I (Michelle) write this book, all sixth graders in my local public school district have been issued tablets for the school year. Books are not issued; paper and pencils are no longer required. Assignments, tests, and projects are all directed toward the students' use of their assigned tablets. Notice the number of older elementary and middle school youth who carry cell phones. It was only a few years ago that you had the option of purchasing a cell phone with a camera built into it. Now there is not a major name-brand cell phone available that does not have photography and videography capabilities as standard features.

How we integrate and use technology in ministry is a reflection of how we love God, love self, and love neighbor. It is an ever-present reality regardless of how we feel about it. Therefore, it is incumbent upon us to understand how people's use and abuse of technology might cause harm to themselves and others.

Cell Phones

Following are some statistics that help us understand the permeation and use of cell phones in our society. (These stats come from the Pew Internet Project related to mobile technology.)

Safe Sanctuaries in a Virtual World

As of May 2013:

- 91% of American adults had a cell phone;
- 56% of American adults had a smart phone; and
- 28% of cell phone owners purchased an Android; 25% purchased an iPhone; 4% purchased a BlackBerry.

Cell phone users engage in all types of activities:

- 82% use their phones to take pictures;
- 80% use their phones to send and receive text messages;
- 56% use their phones to access the Internet;
- 50% use their phones to send and receive e-mails;
- 44% use their phones to record video;
- 43% use their phones to download apps;
- 31% use their phones to look for health or medical information online; and
- 29% use their phones to check bank account balances and do online banking.

Some additional facts about cell phone users:

- 67% of cell phone owners find themselves checking their phones for messages, alerts, or calls—even when they don't notice their phone ringing or vibrating.
- 44% of cell phone owners have slept with their phones next to the bed because they wanted to make sure they didn't miss any calls, text messages, or other updates during the night.
- 29% of owners describe their cell phones as something they "can't imagine living without."
- 55% of adult cell phone owners use the Internet on their mobile phones; nearly double what studies found three years ago.
- 31% of current cell phone Internet users say that they go online using mostly their cell phones, rather than some other device, such as a desktop or laptop computer. Adults make up 17% of these "cell-mostly Internet users."
- 9% of adults have texted a charitable donation from their mobile phones. Mobile giving played an especially prominent role during the aftermath of the January 2010 Haiti earthquake, as individual donors contributed an estimated $43 million to the assistance and reconstruction efforts using the text messaging feature on their cell phones.
- The first-ever in-depth study on mobile donors—which analyzed the "Text to Haiti" campaign after the 2010 earthquake—found that these contributions were often the result of spur-of-the-moment decisions that spread virally through friend networks.

Chapter 3: Basic Procedures for Ministry in a Virtual World

- 74% of Haiti text donors say that donating to the Haiti earthquake relief was the first time they had used their phones' text messaging function to make a donation to an event, cause, or organization.
- 22% had texted a donation of some kind prior to their contribution to Haiti earthquake relief.

Cell phones are a large part of our lives. As with most anything in life, there are both blessings and burdens inherent in this gift of creation. Let's examine the story about Sally and Reverend Jones.

Best Practices and Food for Thought

Cell phone usage: What guidelines have you as an individual, church employee, or church volunteer developed regarding the use of your cell phone?

- *Is it for personal use only? Business use only? Combination of the two?*
- *To whom do you make calls on your cell phone? From whom do you receive calls on your cell phone?*
- *Does anyone know to whom you are speaking outside "official" time?*
- *Does anyone know to whom you are speaking while you are functioning in an official leadership capacity?*

These questions do not imply that you need to start keeping a log of every call made or received. It also does not mean you need to be paranoid about using your cell phone. One of the things that provided opportunity after opportunity for Reverend Jones to act inappropriately was his personal cell phone, which he used in ways that conveyed secrecy rather than honesty, transparency, and accountability.

"Each night Reverend Jones called Sally again." It would have been helpful to Reverend Jones to have his wife serve as an accountability partner. What would it mean to give your spouse access to, without notice, periodically checking your phone for messages sent and received, calls made and calls received? What about simply letting your spouse or roommate know whom you are calling after "business hours" whenever you pick up your phone?

If not your spouse, who else could serve as a trusted accountability partner?

Cell phone stalking: How could you guard against false accusations of cell phone stalking?

- Consider mass texting to groups rather than one-to-one texting.
- Consider face-to-face conversations when the information that needs to be shared is beyond factual information sharing.
- Consider the language (and images) that you use in your texting. Is the language that you use such that if a text were sent to all parents and other leaders of the church, it would not be found objectionable or inappropriate?

> What guidelines have you as an individual, church employee, or church volunteer developed regarding the use of your cell phone?

Sexting

The term *sexting* is a recent addition to our English vocabulary, used to describe the transmission, through texting, of graphic sexual messages or images. Reverend Jones sent sexually explicit images of himself to Sally via his cell phone.

While sexting is not illegal when the image is of a person or people of adult age, it is important to consider the ease with which information and photos are shared via the Internet. Once you send a picture via electronic transmission, you lose the ability to control who sees it, where it is shared, when it is shared, and how it might affect your future.

Sexting is illegal if the photographed image is of any person under adult age. If someone texts you a sexually explicit picture and the person in the photograph is under adult age, you can be considered in possession of child pornography. Additionally, if you receive a sexually explicit picture of a minor and you share that picture with another person, the law may consider charges of distribution of child pornography.

Education Beyond Yourself and Leaders

Parents: It is common for the involvement level of parents to shift as their children age and prepare for adulthood. It is critical that we continue to communicate with parents and other church leaders regarding what is expected from youth leaders:

- *How will youth leadership contact youth?*
- *When? How often?*
- *How will youth leadership communicate with parents?*
- *To whom should the parents speak if they have questions or concerns?*
- *What level of technological expertise do the parents of the youth possess?* Many times youth and children are much more advanced technologically than the average parent or adult.
- *Would it be helpful to provide training to parents in technology and the ways they can help their youth set up safe parameters for online engagement?*

Youth and young adults: Sally found herself in a situation that was unfamiliar and that she was unprepared to address. How do you educate youth and young adults regarding the potential problems related to cell phone use? This situation may have had a very different outcome if Sally had received some education from her parents and the church regarding safe people and places to turn to if she ever encountered a situation online or with technology that made her feel uncomfortable or fearful.

Children are being exposed to the whole concept of sexuality while still very young. Most schools are beginning to address issues of sexuality, adolescence, and sexual relationships as early as fourth grade. Children in the fourth grade are normally eight or nine years old. Sexual misconduct in any form, including sexual harassment, sexual abuse, and the experiences of sexualized behavior by others, is a concept that is difficult for eight- and nine-year-old children to process in their cognitive concrete

Chapter 3: Basic Procedures for Ministry in a Virtual World

thinking. Such concepts need to be revisited often with children as they grow toward adulthood. Sally was experiencing sexual harassment as well as uninvited sexualized behavior that was not only unethical but also illegal. Yet Sally did not know that was going on in her situation. She only knew she did not like what she was experiencing, she was scared, and she did not know what to do when her request to be left alone was not received and followed. Although Sally knew her parents loved and cared for her, she was too embarrassed to talk to them about the whole situation.

This situation was further exacerbated by the fact that the alleged perpetrator was a known and trusted leader in her church. Consider the following:

- *In what ways do you encourage children and youth to have close trusted relationships with adults in the church?*
- *How do you try to ensure that these relationships are bound in sacred trust?*
- *In what ways do you give those in less powerful positions (youth, elderly persons, and children) permission to speak up when injustices or abuse occurs?*

> We all need a place in which we can be our authentic selves, find nurture and grace, and be held accountable for the ways we are living as children of God.

Care for Ministry Leaders, Including Yourself

Regardless of whether you are paid or a volunteer, the only person serving in a leadership capacity, or the leader of many leaders, caring for yourself is vital to healthy and effective ministry. We all need a place in which we can be our authentic selves, find nurture and grace, and be held accountable for the ways we are living as children of God.

Leadership Expectations

In this particular scenario, it might have been helpful to Reverend Jones as well as the other adult youth leaders to have a designated time for gathering and experiencing spiritual growth as a leadership team. The leadership team could also provide a safe environment in which concerns about youth or adults could be raised for conversation, clarification, and processing. It would be helpful for the leadership team (both paid and volunteer) to establish a written covenant stating leadership expectations, including expectations for nurturing relationships with students via cell phones, social media, and so on. A sample "Youth Ministry Leadership Covenant" can be found in the Sample Forms section of this book.

Understanding Power

Reverend Jones was the person in this relationship with more power. He was the pastor. He was the leader of a group of which Sally was a part. The scenario tells us that Sally asked Reverend Jones to not call her. He continued. What Reverend Jones did not understand was that when Sally said no, explicitly or implicitly, he had a responsibility to respect her decision. Reverend Jones abused his power by using his position as pastor and leader to continue contacting Sally. He used his position of authority to bribe her to serve as a Bible study leader in order to get a good recommendation for college, and to contact her at orientation. It is always the responsibility of the one with greater power to be aware of and govern the ways in which that power is appropriately displayed in a relationship.

Personal Boundaries

Reverend Jones prided himself on always being "available" to the youth, staff, parents, and volunteers. Even Jesus took personal time for prayer, reflection, rest, and retreat. All of us need time away. Encourage leaders, including yourself, to take and honor sabbath rest. Ask someone to hold you accountable for honoring the sabbath.

Establish personal boundaries for yourself and your family regarding cell phone usage. Create a "no phone zone." In my (Michelle's) home, phones are not allowed at the kitchen table, and my children are not permitted to leave the table to answer a ringing phone or to read or respond to a text or e-mail. My children also have a "phone curfew" that coincides with their bedtime. They are not allowed to keep their phones in their bedrooms overnight.

My cell phone remains on all day and all night. I do not make calls, except in emergency situations, after 9 p.m. I screen all calls that I receive after 5 p.m.

Social Media

Cell phones are only one small piece of the multimedia pie. The Internet is another large component. Three of the world's most popular brands online are social media–related: Facebook, YouTube, and Wikipedia. A social medium is any electronic form of communication that is designed to create online interactive communities for the purposes of sharing information, opinions, messages, and ideas in a variety of different forms. Social media can include, but are not limited to, popular communities such as Facebook, Twitter, Instagram, Flickr, Vine, YouTube, Wikipedia, Blogger, and Pinterest. Social media are quickly becoming mainstream forms of communication. We find and will continue to find ourselves engaging in ministry and equipping others for discipleship and ministry in the world through social media. Just as interpersonal, face-to-face relationships must be monitored and balanced with boundaries, so too does our use of social media.

In our implementation of technology, it is imperative that we continue to consider the boundaries we establish, the ways we respect other people's boundaries, and the dynamic that exists when a person is not physically in front of us for conversation and engagement.

People continue to use social media in a variety of ways. Pew Research Center's Internet and American Life Project gathered some interesting statistics:[1]

- 67% of adults surveyed use Facebook.
- 16% of adults use Twitter.
- 15% of adults use Pinterest.

Chapter 3: Basic Procedures for Ministry in a Virtual World

- 13% of adults use Instagram.
- 6% of adults use Tumblr.
- Facebook still tops social networks as the most used.
- 17% of computer time is spent on Facebook.
- The second-largest social media outlet is Blogger.
- Twitter is now the third-largest social network.
- Pinterest grew 1,047% and is now used more than Google+ or Myspace.
- LinkedIn usage remained the same.
- The total time spent online in the United States is up 21%.
- Social networks still dominate Internet usage, garnering 20% of PC time and 30% of mobile time.
- Knowing someone was the top reason for communicating online, followed by "interested in keeping up" and mutual friends.
- Other reasons included quality of profile photo and a person's physical attractiveness, both of which were reasons more for men than women.
- Professional benefits were also a consideration, including access to business networks and a person's number of connections.[2]
- 100 hours of video are uploaded to YouTube every minute.[3]
- Pinterest has reached 70 million registered users. 71% of Pinterest users are from within the USA.[4]

Reality vs. Perceived Reality: One of the greatest problems with our engagement in online communities is that we quickly lose perspective of the difference between reality and perceived reality. What do I mean by that? Without the ability to engage all of our senses, as would be the case in face-to-face personal relationships, we often rely on only the sense of sight and our emotions to make decisions during interactions in cyber communities. This often leads to impaired judgment and a skewed ability to separate truth and fiction.

Our actions and reactions in the cyberworld are often instantaneous and unbridled because we do not have the accountability of someone's physical presence, facial expression, or words to hold us in check. Without much thought, a post, text, e-mail, instant message, or status update is sent with a simple click of a button and, more often than not, cannot be retracted. The information will be "out there" forever and is a reflection of the sender's character and identity as a person, a leader in ministry, and a child of God.

Our online actions and reactions are often made less justifiable because of two misperceptions:

Misperception #1—Perception is reality: We are, by nature, trusting people. If we receive an e-mail, text, or Facebook message from someone stating he is John Doe, we presume it to be from the *real* John Doe. Social networking and other forms of technology are challenging our understandings of perception and reality. It would be very easy for someone (who is *not* John Doe) to find a picture of John Doe on the Internet, copy it as his profile picture, place John Doe's name beside the picture, and use John Doe's profile in a variety of negative and disparaging ways.

Our natural ability to survive is linked to our basic senses—the natural instinct of when to fight and when to take flight, the ability to separate fact from fiction, and the ability to determine honesty and dishonesty. Without the benefit of face-to-face interactions, however, our basic senses are at a definite disadvantage. Online engagement is making it difficult for us to determine when something is safe, right, and pure. Therefore, it is incumbent upon us to do the work necessary to make sure that what we see is real and appropriate.

Misperception #2—If it feels private online, it is private: Even though something might feel private (you and a screen and one other person), remember that any information you put on the Internet, regardless of whether it is through a PC or a mobile device (blogs, e-mails, status updates, photos, videos, tweets, and sometimes even texts), can easily become accessible for public consumption. Others can copy your information, attribute it to you (or not), and place it in other forums and social community sites. It is becoming more and more common for prospective employees, even college and university admission offices, to employ the Internet to gain a better understanding of a potential employee or student. Every time you use the Internet or are identified by others using the Internet, you are adding to your online portfolio and public profile.

Representatives of Christ

It is also important to remember that as leaders in the church, we don't represent just ourselves; we represent church leaders everywhere. And more than that, we are the living representatives of Christ in the world. Our behavior, the way we conduct ourselves as leaders in ministry, is a projected reflection of other clergy and church leaders. We are all role models and spiritual leaders—like it or not, people judge all of us by the actions of One—the One whom they know and love and trust. Think about this: If you are a clergy member, when are you not a minister, a representative of Christ to the world? If you are a laity member, when are you not a disciple of Jesus Christ, a witness of the good news of the Gospels? We have been adopted by God through Jesus Christ. We are a part of an eternal family. Our witness and faith are not a coat that we can take on and off. They are an integral part of who we are. So, even if we are not in the church or actively serving as ministry leader when we are utilizing social media, we are forever and at all times disciples of Christ, children of God, and representatives of Christ to the world. How should this affect our actions, language, and interactions in the virtual world?

When our boundaries begin to erode in the virtual world, a snowball of sorts begins to form at the top of a proverbial mountain. Each time we rationalize and say yes in our hearts to boundary-crossing behavior, the snowball gathers strength and grows larger in its downhill journey. It is of utmost importance that we stop and consider whether our behavior is acceptable and appropriate before acting.

Chapter 3: Basic Procedures for Ministry in a Virtual World

Utilizing Social Media in Ministry

Consider again the story of Reverend Jones. It was his practice to use the social networking site Facebook to develop relationships with youth. He became "friends" with all the youth. Establishing relationships with others through social media sites is not a bad thing. There are many positive aspects to online communities. Here are just a few:

- Social media are the ways members of the younger generations are connecting with one another on a daily basis.

- Conversations can occur and information can be relayed in real time.

- Information can reach a large number of people in a very short amount of time.

- Communication is not dependent on being in a particular geographic location.

- Social media create communities and connect people with common interests much more quickly than a scheduled weekly or monthly ministry gathering.

- Social media provide avenues whereby work and conversation can continue long after the "official" conversation, appointment, or gathering has occurred.

Some points to consider in utilizing social media in ministry:

1. Do you reach out to all participants in ministry through social media, or do you pick and choose the people you will engage with through these networks? Are these decisions made on a case-by-case basis? Have you created guidelines to aid you in making these types of decisions?

2. Consider again the power you possess in your role as a ministry leader. Is it possible that people may feel as though they can't ignore or block you from their network because of your position? What would it mean if you encouraged others to invite you to join their "community" rather than you asking them to join yours? Best practice would be to accept all invites from those who are a part of your ministry area and/or to invite all who are a part of your ministry area.

3. This scenario does not describe the contents of Reverend Jones's social networking site. Did his personal page also contain work connections? Was it a church-related page or group? Consider establishing clear boundaries around your social media activity. It would be helpful to have an open social media community for the youth group. This way all youth, adult leaders, and other church staff could see what was going on in terms of events, conversations, plans, and people engaged in the ministry. You could also create a Pinterest board or an Instagram account in the name of the church or youth ministry of which all the participants could become "followers."

Why would this be helpful?

- There would be no secrecy. Youth, youth counselors, parents, church staff, and anyone else who was interested could see what was happening in this area of ministry.

Notes

Safe Sanctuaries in a Virtual World

- Clear boundaries would be set; the page, board, blog, or account would be in the name of the church or ministry and established for only that purpose, not personal use. People would know where to go for information regarding any upcoming activities, events, schedule changes, and so on. Power is recognized and equalized. Open groups, pages, accounts, and the like that are created in the name of the organization and used for the appropriate purposes of the organization allow people the choice of whether or not to be a part. There is not pressure to say yes to the pastor because an invitation has been sent or to initiate a relationship with a leader of ministry if you are not comfortable doing that online.

Cyberbullying and Cyberstalking

Reverend Jones began using the private message feature found on Facebook to reach out to Sally when she did not respond to his texts. Utilizing private message features, one-to-one texts, and private accounts places us, as leaders in the church or the church's ministry, in a precarious position whereby our ethics, integrity, and honesty may be called into question.

Why did Reverend Jones begin using private messaging? He was not getting any response to his texts, and he did not want the world to know that he was pursuing Sally. In this particular instance, Reverend Jones may also have been in violation of bullying or stalking via the Internet, more commonly referred to as cyberbullying or cyberstalking.

Both cyberbullying and cyberstalking are serious forms of online harassment. Cyberstalking and cyberbullying are similar in nature, as both involve sending repeated, unsolicited, and harassing messages and/or images.

Cyberbullying occurs when someone uses the Internet (including e-mail, social networking sites, texts, websites, gaming sites, chat rooms, or blogs) or other electronic means to threaten physical harm or cause psychological distress to someone else. Cyberbullying can involve teasing, intimidation, threats, disparaging remarks about a person's race, ethnicity, religion, or sexuality, disclosure of personal, humiliating, or embarrassing information about the other person without permission to share, fraudulent use of his or her Internet accounts, or language that is degrading or insulting. Cyberbullying becomes much more serious when the motivations and tactics employed include an obsession with the particular person being bullied.

Cyberstalking includes harassing behavior that is repeated over an extended period of time for the purposes of control, manipulation, submission, and/or access to the person and his or her life. In the eyes of the law, cyberstalking is a more serious offense than cyberbullying. Cyberbullying may be a onetime event whereas cyberstalking involves a pattern of events and/or behavior that creates extreme emotional distress over an extended period of time. While laws vary from state to state, all states are recognizing the harm created through cyberbullying and cyberstalking. Each state is taking appropriate measures to use existing laws as well as to create new laws to address the problems of cyberbullying and cyberstalking.

Chapter 3: Basic Procedures for Ministry in a Virtual World

Privacy and Secrecy

Whenever you use any feature of social networking that allows you more "privacy" with another person, ask yourself why this is the appropriate avenue to take. Is it because you are sharing or conversing about something that would not be appropriate otherwise? Is there any element of secrecy that is a motivating factor in this decision?

Not all private messaging or one-to-one texting is bad. Sometimes I (Michelle) use private messaging to share with someone my home address. My home address is not something I want the world to know via social media. Sometimes I use one-to-one texting to gather information that is needed for my ministry—what hospital has a church member been taken to after an emergency has occurred? What time does some program begin? Informational sharing is appropriate. The building of unsuitable relationships or any type of bullying or stalking is not.

Best Practices for Prevention of Social Media Misconduct

The best strategy for the prevention of social media misconduct—or even a social media disaster—in your context of ministry is the use of education, conversation, covenant, and accountability.

Education: Develop a social media use policy for the ministry, and then provide all employees and volunteers with sufficient training to properly implement the policy. A strong social media use policy will balance the ministry's need for communication with the need for upholding the ministry's values of respect for all persons. As an employer, the church or ministry has the authority to develop and adopt social media use policies for the protection of its reputation. The church expects employees and volunteers to follow church policies, and it can carry out consequences up to and including dismissal for failure to follow the policies. Most companies in the secular arena have implemented such policies. We hear news stories nearly every day of an employee's misuse of a company's social media and the consequences to the company as well as the consequences to the employee.

The National Labor Relations Board is working to provide guidance to secular employers regarding what to include or emphasize in social media use policies. The guidance includes a sample policy that can be found at the NLRB website, www.nlrb.gov. We have provided sample social media use policies for both volunteers and employees in the Sample Forms section of this resource.

Drawing from the secular model policies, here are several items our ministries need to include in social media use policies:

- Note that in social media and online communications, the dividing line between public and private information, as well as between personal and professional information, may be difficult to discern. Whenever any one of us identifies ourselves as an employee/volunteer of the [church or ministry] online, we are connected to other employees, members, volunteers, supporters, and prospective members. It is important to ensure that any posted content associated with you is consistent with the church's values and standards.

> The best strategy for the prevention of social media misconduct—or even a social media disaster—in your context of ministry is the use of education, conversation, covenant, and accountability.

- Be respectful of others. The church's social media will not be used to post and disseminate discriminatory comments or content, harassment, threats of violence, criminal acts or behavior, abuse of any type, bullying, hate speech, or demeaning comments.

- The church's social media will not be used to share, reveal, or disseminate confidential or proprietary information, including financial information, counseling information, or information to do with legal matters.

- No posts of pornography, vulgarity, obscenity, nudity, or partial nudity in text, photos, or videos will be allowed for any purpose at any time.

- Only specific employees are authorized to speak on behalf of the church in an official capacity. Therefore, be sure to designate your postings and/or comments as your own and not those of the church or ministry. When making your own comments, the church expects that you will use your personal e-mail/online address, not the church's. The church prefers that your personal posts be accompanied by a statement that the postings are your own and do not reflect the church's (or ministry's) opinions or values.

- Postings deemed inappropriate by the church leadership (as defined by the church or ministry context) will be removed.

- Before posting anything, remember that you—the employee or volunteer—are responsible for the post's content. Before you click Send, take a break—get a cup of coffee or tea—even save the draft and come back to it the next day. Do not post in haste or anger. Consider the consequences of the post, and restrain yourself if there is a chance you are not being reasonable. Remember that even comments you think you are making anonymously can potentially be traced back to you or the church. Privacy settings are not foolproof and cannot be relied on to protect identity. If you have any doubt about the validity or reasonableness of the post, don't send it without consulting the business manager or pastor or ministry leader.

- Posting the church/ministry logo or trademarked images is prohibited without advance permission.

Conversation: Have conversations as a staff and as a ministry team about the following:

- *What types of social media will your ministry use and why?*
- *Who will be the administrator(s)?*
- *What, if any, filters will be put in place to screen content?*
- *What is appropriate and inappropriate content on these sites?*
- *What expectations does the church personnel committee have of the staff regarding use of social media?*
- *What expectations does the church leadership have of the lay leaders regarding use of social media?*

Chapter 3: Basic Procedures for Ministry in a Virtual World

- *What are the known concerns regarding the utilization of social media as a major component in your ministry?*

Covenant: As members of the body of Christ, we are called to be in covenantal relationship with one another. Once conversations have been shared regarding expectations of staff and ministry leaders, it is best practice to codify those expectations through a written covenant that is signed by all persons. The exercise of writing a covenant allows misunderstandings to be worked out, clarifications to occur, and clearly defined boundaries to be established.

Accountability: What will the consequences be if someone breaks the covenant your church has agreed to uphold? How do the accountability practices differ between paid staff and volunteer leaders?

Accountability is not about judgment or condemnation. It is not about "big brother" watching us, or a lack of trust. As humans we have an incredible ability to deceive ourselves. We are capable of rationalizing almost anything, especially if each individual indiscretion and choice that is made is a small compromise in integrity. Accountability places us in a posture of humility in which we are able to see ourselves exactly as we are, as imperfect humans who have lapses in judgment and choose inappropriate behavior for the sake of selfish gain. Accountability is a gift from God that aids us in helping one another strive more and more to be like Christ. The gift of accountability is needed to protect us from ourselves, much more so than to protect us from others. Consider again some of the stories of accountability, love, and grace found throughout the scriptures: God holding Adam and Eve accountable for their actions, the story of King David and Bathsheba, Jesus and the woman at the well, and the many times Paul speaks in the Epistles about the importance of accountability for the growth and edification of the individual members of the church as well as the corporate body, just to name a few.

Social media are tools whereby effective and fruitful ministry may grow and be nurtured. Although these tools can aid us and increase the scope of contact and connection as well as the breadth of people who may be touched by our ministry offerings, social media cannot be the source or foundation of ministry. Our foundation is Jesus Christ. Social media are creations of human ingenuity that provide for us one more way to express and proclaim the good news of the gospel of Jesus Christ. We are called to use social media with care, consideration, intentionality, and a Christlike spirit.

Notes

Chapter 4

Pornography and Obscenity

> God said, "Let us make humankind in our image, according to our likeness; and let them have dominion over the fish of the sea, and over the birds of the air, and over the cattle, and over all the wild animals of the earth, and over every creeping thing that creeps upon the earth." So God created humankind in his image, in the image of God he created them; male and female he created them. God blessed them, and God said to them, "Be fruitful and multiply, and fill the earth and subdue it; and have dominion over the fish of the sea and over the birds of the air and over every living thing that moves upon the earth." . . . God saw everything that he had made, and indeed, it was very good.
>
> —Genesis 1:26-28, 31

The Gift of Sex

Created in the image of God, we were created male and female. We were commanded by God to "be fruitful and increase in number." God gave to humanity the gift of sex. Along with the expressed command to increase in number, sexuality was given to humanity as an expression of our intimate connection with one another as cocreators with God. It is the distortion and the perversion of this gift of sex and the expressions of our sexuality that lead to the brokenness many experience through the abuse of and addiction to sexual behaviors that include pornography.

Imagine the following scenario: A couple in your congregation has asked to meet with you regarding their son, who participates in the youth ministry of the church. At the meeting the parents inform you of the following event:

Their son was helping to prepare for Sunday-evening youth group. He needed to type out the words to some songs on the computer. He asked to use the youth director's computer to do this task. She allowed him to go into her office and have access to her computer. While he was using the computer, he came across adult pornographic pictures that had been downloaded to this particular computer. He completed his original task, closed down the computer, and continued with his preparations. Later that same evening he confided in his parents about this whole situation.

Safe Sanctuaries in a Virtual World

The next morning you receive two more phone calls from other parents who have learned about the pictures found on the computer and are demanding to know what you are going to do about it.

- *What is your immediate thought?*
- *What will be your initial response to the parents?*
- *What will be your initial response to the youth director?*
- *What will be your initial response to the male student?*
- *What will be your initial response to the other parents who know of this allegation?*
- *What will be your initial response to the greater congregation?*
- *What other people will you draw into this conversation? Why?*
- *What procedures instituted by your church or your staff are in place to aid you in times such as these?*

In this particular scenario, it turned out that the youth director was found innocent of all allegations. The young man mistakenly stumbled onto a porn site when he was looking for graphics to add to the song lyric slides he was creating. In his attempts to close out and leave the porn site, several images were downloaded. Upon discovering the pornographic pictures in the clip art folder of the computer, he tried to remove them unsuccessfully. Embarrassed by the situation and fearful of getting in trouble, the youth fabricated the story.

The pastor got to the bottom of the story when he was able to sit and speak with the young man alone, without his parents or the youth director in the room. The church had a password protection system on their computer server to record all actions and time stamps of downloads. The young man was signed on to the computer as "guest" via the youth director's computer, and the time stamps were in alignment with his time on the computer.

The pastor was able to respond to the other parents in a timely and appropriate manner without divulging the whole story or causing further embarrassment to the young man. The young man was required to write a letter of apology to the youth director. After some time passed, the youth and their parents were invited to participate in a church-sponsored workshop focused on sex, porn, and the Internet.

Pornography

Online pornography is an area of growing concern for our families, faith communities, and clergy. The ease of access to the Internet through mobile devices, computers, and the television has opened a new window into exploration, exploitation, and addiction that are having grave consequences on those involved and affected. Statistics have shown a rise in the use of pornography in our society, with revenue from pornographic materials growing each year. In 2001 the revenue from video, Internet, pay-per-view, and magazines was estimated conservatively at $3.9 billion.[1] In 2005 the revenue generated from video sales and rentals, Internet, cable, pay-per-view, phone sex, mobile

> God gave to humanity the gift of sex. Along with the expressed command to increase in number, sexuality was given to humanity as an expression of our intimate connection with one another as cocreators with God.

Chapter 4: Pornography and Obscenity

access, dance clubs, novelties, and magazines was $12.62 billion. In 2006 the amount of revenue generated rose to $13.33 billion.[2] Today the statistics are even more difficult to capture due to the amount of video piracy, free websites, and online porn bulletin boards developing throughout the world. Suffice it to say that the pornography industry is continuing to rake in billions of dollars. These dollars are indicative of the number of people accessing, buying, and utilizing the pornographic materials. Large numbers are often hard to understand. Breaking the numbers down a bit makes the scope of the problem much clearer.

There are 4.2 million pornographic websites. This is 12% of the total of all websites.[3] Every second . . .

- $3,075.64 is being spent on pornography; and
- 28,258 Internet viewers are viewing pornography.[4]

Children's Exposure to Pornography

According to some statistical reports regarding children in the United States, the average age of first exposure to pornography is eleven, with 90% of eight- to sixteen-year-olds stating that they have viewed pornography online, most while doing homework.[5] In a national survey of youth utilizing the Internet, most kids who reported unwanted exposure were ages thirteen to seventeen. There was still a sizable group of ten- and eleven-year-olds reporting unwanted exposure—17% of the boys in the group and 16% of the girls.[6] The use of and access to the Internet, through cell phones, tablets, computers, and other portable electronic devices, is pervasive in the lives of young children. Couple that with the fact that pornographic sites are extremely easy to access, both when they are sought and when they are accidentally stumbled upon, and it is no wonder that the children are viewing pornography at such a young age. Many pornographic-site developers are utilizing key search words that are child-friendly, such as *White House*, *Pokemon*, and *Barbie*.[7]

Pornography and Marriage

The American Academy of Matrimonial Lawyers (divorce attorneys) reported that the most significant factors in divorce were related to online activity:

- 68% involved one party meeting a new love interest over the Internet.
- 56% involved "one party having an obsessive interest in pornographic websites."
- 47% involved "spending excessive time on the computer."
- 33% involved spending excessive time in chat rooms (a commonly sexualized forum).[8]

Richard Barry, president of the association, said, "Pornography had an almost nonexistent role in divorce just seven or eight years ago."[9]

Notes

Safe Sanctuaries in a Virtual World

Addiction to Pornography

For a large portion of our society, including many seated in our congregations and living in our communities, there is a deep struggle with pornography and pornographic materials. Regardless of our faith practices, religious expressions, and faithfulness, even those who express a high level of commitment to God struggle:

- 53% of men belonging to the Christian group Promise Keepers reported having viewed pornography in the last week.[10]
- 47% of Christians say that pornography is a problem in the home.[11]
- 50% of all Christian men and 20% of all Christian women are addicted to pornography.[12]
- 60% of the women who answered the survey admitted to having significant struggles with lust; 40% admitted to being involved in sexual sin in the past year; and 20% of the churchgoing female participants struggled with looking at pornography on an ongoing basis.[13]
- In 2003, one out of every six women, or 17% of the population, including those who identified themselves as Christians, struggled with an addiction to pornography.[14] In 2006, according to another poll, 20% of Christian women reported an addiction to porn.[15]
- More than 80% of women who have an addiction to porn take it off-line. Women, far more than men, are likely to act out their behaviors in real life by having multiple partners, casual sex, or affairs.[16]

Once thought of as only a "man's issue," it is evident from studies being conducted that the number of females accessing pornography is also quite large. It is important to note that there are more publications and websites available for men than for women, and the greatest amount of research to date has been focused on men. Statistically speaking, we also know that men view pornography more often than women. While studies are beginning to show that women also use pornography, we are learning that because their behavior usually continues off-line, it is less able to be calculated for statistical purposes. Some of this statistical data may also be attributed to the fact that men are more visual; that is, they are more easily excited by what they see, while women are more excited by the sense of touch. Likewise, males are often initially attracted to a person's physical characteristics, while females are often initially attracted to relational qualities exhibited in a person.

The first thought of many is that pornography is used for sexual arousal and personal pleasure. More often than not, however, the use of pornography has little to do with sexual gratification or "any erotic reaction to the sexual nature of the image."[17] The use of pornography has more to do with fantasy, power, and control. Quite often, pornography is used as a way to suppress a feeling of loss of power, to fulfill a fantasy or dream, or to make one's self feel good, emotionally, spiritually, and physically. The desire for power, control, and fantasy fulfillment becomes a sexual response because of the sexual medium that was sought to fulfill the need.

We are sexual beings. God created us to enjoy the pleasures of procreation and intimacy with one another. We are wired for connection. Our brains actually create

---

> We are wired for connection. Our brains actually create pathways as we relate with one another. These pathways grow deeper and wider as we grow and become more social creatures, aiding us and directing our ways of relating.

Chapter 4: Pornography and Obscenity

pathways as we relate with one another. These pathways grow deeper and wider as we grow and become more social creatures, aiding us and directing our ways of relating. When we meet someone, our brains immediately begin to go down the path that has been created for relationships.

When a person begins to engage in pornography, a pathway is created in the brain. As the pornographic activity continues, that pathway automatically begins to respond when the next image, erotic material, or sensual touch is encountered. The brain becomes conditioned to believe that what is seen and experienced is appropriate and right. This slowly becomes the person's "default" behavior for relating with others. Furthermore, the brain produces a variety of different hormones (dopamine, serotonin, norepinephrine, and oxytocin) that automatically link a "high" and good feeling with the pornographic and sexual materials. Feelings of powerlessness, lack of control, or low self-worth lead to the desire to return to those same stimuli to receive the "high" and continue on in life. Over time, it is possible to become desensitized to this same behavior and therefore turn to more and more hard-core pornography to fulfill the perceived need for self-worth, power, or control.[18]

While there are many different beliefs regarding the depth of personal harm that is caused by the use of pornography, nearly every study done has made it clear that porn does have adverse effects, and these adverse effects go beyond those who are involved in the production of pornography and the observer.

Studies have also concluded that the effects of porn usage are quite detrimental in terms of social demeanor and emotional well-being:[19]

- Pornography depersonalizes attitudes toward those who are portrayed as the objects of desire. One tends to start viewing others as sexually desired objects rather than spiritual or emotional beings. (This can have a major negative effect on the way we relate to one another socially and pastorally.)
- Sexually explicit and suggestive multimedia have a huge impact on our conceptions and practice of sexual relationships within intimate relationships and marriages.
- Pornography often results in infidelity, express marital distress, and the risk of separation and divorce.
- Viewing pornography often results in an increased appetite for more graphic types of pornography and sexual activity associated with abusive, illegal, or unsafe practices.
- Those viewing pornography often experience decreased marital intimacy and sexual satisfaction with their spouses.
- Pornography contributes to the devaluation of monogamy, marriage, and child-rearing.

According to the *Journal of Adolescent Health*, prolonged exposure to pornography leads to the following:

- An exaggerated perception of sexual activity in society
- Diminished trust between intimate couples

Notes

Safe Sanctuaries in a Virtual World

- The abandonment of the hope of sexual monogamy
- Belief that promiscuity is the natural state
- Belief that abstinence and sexual inactivity are unhealthy
- Cynicism about love or the need for affection between sexual partners
- Belief that marriage is sexually confining
- Lack of attraction to family and child-raising[20]

Why Is Pornography Such a Problem for Clergy?

Given how pervasive the problem is in the general population, one may still be left wondering why this is such a problem for our clergy. Clergy are not immune to this struggle. It is a problem that we are seeing both male and female clergy struggle to overcome. Being human themselves, clergy and licensed pastors also wrestle with appropriate expressions of sexuality and often find themselves turning toward and becoming addicted to pornography. Many will argue that this is the fastest-growing problem facing our clergy today. Recent empirical research conducted by the Hope and Healing Institute found that 33% of pastors have deliberately used the Internet to view pornography.[21] Additionally, according to *Christianity Today*,

- 51% of pastors say cyberporn is a possible temptation
- 37% say cyber-based pornography is a current struggle
- 4 in 10 pastors have visited a pornographic site
- a survey of evangelical Protestant clergy in 2001 also found that 40% of those responding struggled with pornography[22]

In March 2002, Rick Warren's Pastors.com website conducted a survey on the porn use of 1,351 pastors: 54% of the pastors had viewed Internet pornography within the last year, and 30% of those had visited pornographic sites within the last thirty days.

Many pastors consume themselves with the role of caring for others and thereby neglect caring for themselves. There is a deep dichotomy between preaching and actually practicing the advice "Take time for sabbath to rest and renew your spirit." Personal needs that go unmet appropriately are much more susceptible to being met in inappropriate ways.

This problem is further exacerbated by pastors who

- are often in churches or appointments that are isolating, either geographically or professionally;
- have feelings of loneliness;
- lack supporting and encouraging peers;
- experience intense expectations, albeit unrealistic, that many congregations place upon their pastors;

Chapter 4: Pornography and Obscenity

- have a predisposed nature to be workaholics and "people pleasers";
- experience minimal personal support; or
- were raised in a culture that has bred the understanding that sex and sexuality are not to be discussed or even considered as appropriate topics for discussion, especially by our clergy.

Already emotionally vulnerable, pastors find themselves in a physical work environment that actually intensifies the problem. Pastors spend much of the day in their offices

- alone;
- unsupervised;
- with self-determined schedules;
- with easy access to the Internet; and
- with no system of consistent accountability.

There is often no designated person, within or beyond the church, to monitor Internet access, check recently visited sites, or monitor the use by the clergy of church- or agency-issued technology. Rather than searching for the careful balance that must exist between accountability practices and "policing" one another, we choose to pretend that this problem does not exist, and therefore, we do not address it or even try to understand it.

The problem is further clouded when we begin to examine the differences between secular/civil legal definitions and the ethical and denominational standards that govern our sacred relationships with one another.

What the Laws Say about Pornography and Obscenity

Let's be clear about our terminology. *Merriam-Webster's Collegiate Dictionary* (eleventh edition) defines *pornography* as: "1: the depiction of erotic behavior (as in pictures or writing) intended to cause sexual excitement" and "2: material (as in books or a photograph) that depicts erotic behavior and is intended to cause sexual excitement."

Merriam-Webster's online *Concise Encyclopedia* defines *obscenity* as an "act, utterance, writing, or illustration that is deemed deeply offensive according to contemporary community standards of morality and decency."

Every state has assigned legal definitions of *pornography* and *obscenity* in its statutes following the holdings of the United States Supreme Court. The standard articulated there for what constitutes obscenity includes three factors. Material is considered obscene if (1) the average person, applying local community standards, looking at the work in its entirety, finds that it appeals to the prurient interest; (2) the work describes or depicts, in an obviously offensive way, sexual conduct or excretory functions; and (3) the work as a whole lacks serious literary, artistic, political, or scientific value.

Notes

Notes

Safe Sanctuaries in a Virtual World

As a specific example, Georgia state law section 16-12-80 defines material as obscene if:

1. to the average person, applying contemporary community standards, taken as a whole, it predominantly appeals to the prurient interest, that is, a shameful or morbid interest in nudity, sex, or excretion;

2. the material taken as a whole lacks serious literary, artistic, political, or scientific value; and

3. the material depicts or describes, in a patently offensive way, sexual conduct specifically defined in subparagraphs (A) through (E) of this paragraph:

    (A) acts of sexual intercourse, heterosexual or homosexual, normal or perverted, actual or simulated;

    (B) acts of masturbation;

    (C) acts involving excretory functions or lewd exhibition of the genitals;

    (D) acts of bestiality or the fondling of sex organs of animals; or

    (E) sexual acts of flagellation, torture, or other violence indicating a sadomasochistic sexual relationship.

The United States Supreme Court has addressed the questions of what is pornography and what is protected speech under the US Constitution. In what has become perhaps the most often remembered opinion on obscenity and pornography, Justice Potter Stewart wrote in 1964 (regarding *Jacobellis v. Ohio*; 378 U.S. 184), "I shall not today attempt further to define the kinds of material I understand to be embraced within that shorthand description ["hard-core pornography"]; and perhaps I could never succeed in intelligibly doing so. But I know it when I see it, and the motion picture involved in this case is not that." The movie involved in this case was a film called *The Lovers* and involved adults. Thus, in state and federal laws, pornography in itself is not always illegal to possess as long as those in the pornographic material are of adult age. The laws of most states are based on a widely accepted definition of pornography which defines it as any sexually explicit material that portrays violence, abuse, coercion, domination, humiliation, or degradation for the purpose of arousal." Our laws severely punish not only those who produce pornography, especially child pornography, but also those who provide pornographic materials to minors. The sentences for such crimes range from one to thirty years.

Obscenity and *pornography* are terms frequently used together. Obscenity, as defined above, is often used to designate certain materials as being illegal to possess. There are criminal penalties for possessing obscene materials. Often referred to as "hard-core porn," obscene pornographic material is defined in many states as "materials of a sexual nature that are beyond what the majority of society will tolerate." In the framework of state and federal laws, obscene pornographic materials often are those including images of children, but not always.

For us the questions might include: *Should we, or can we, encourage the use of movies, videos, books, and so on in our secular world as points of reference for education concerning, debate about, or learning the dangers and consequences of pornography?* Some

Chapter 4: Pornography and Obscenity

sources that I have recently received questions about include *The Black Swan* (movie); *Game of Thrones* (book and television series); and *Fifty Shades of Grey* (books).

Other questions include: Would such items best be used in an online study forum or face-to-face? What would be the minimum age of study group participants?

When we in the church must evaluate a movie, video, image, story, or book, we can find guidance in the legal world. The case law since *Jacobellis v. Ohio* has led to the development of a framework within which to determine whether or not something is obscene. First, we must ask whether the average person, applying local community standards and looking at the work in its entirety, would find that it appealed to the prurient interest. A problem we encounter is that as a result of the increasing prevalence of sexually explicit material and its infiltration into our daily lives through advertisements, social media, and print media, our society is becoming increasingly accustomed to images once considered inappropriate. Our community standard is changing without us realizing it. Next, we must ask whether the work describes or depicts, in a patently offensive way, sexual conduct or excretory functions defined by state law. Finally, we must ask whether the work as a whole lacks "serious literary, artistic, political, or scientific value." All fifty states have put laws in place using their own form of this basic framework. You can find the statutes for your state in the statutory code, usually on the website of the state legislature.

In ministries, our answers to the questions above may be somewhat different from the answers a jury would render. We have the freedom to develop answers that are true to our beliefs.

The United Methodist Church has affirmed the following:

- Sexuality is God's good gift to all persons. We call everyone to responsible stewardship of this sacred gift.

- Although all persons are sexual beings whether or not they are married, sexual relations are affirmed only within the covenant of monogamous, heterosexual marriage.

- We deplore all forms of the commercialization, abuse, and exploitation of sex. . . . The Church should support the family in providing age-appropriate education regarding sexuality to children, youth and adults.[23]

Furthermore, the church states:

> Violent, disrespectful, or abusive sexual expressions do not confirm sexuality as God's good gift. We reject all sexual expressions that damage the humanity God has given us as birthright, and we affirm only that sexual expression that enhances that same humanity. We believe that sexual relations where one or both partners are exploitative, abusive, or promiscuous are beyond the parameters of acceptable Christian behavior and are ultimately destructive to individuals, families and the social order. We deplore all forms of the commercialization and exploitation of sex, with the consequent cheapening and degradation of human personality. To lose freedom and be sold by someone else for sexual purposes is a form of slavery, and we denounce such business and support the abused and their right to freedom.[24]

Notes

Safe Sanctuaries in a Virtual World

In response to this understanding of sexuality as God's good gift, the church now affirms that "misconduct of a sexual nature is a chargeable offense, for both laity and clergy. Chargeable offenses include: child abuse, sexual abuse, sexual misconduct, sexual harassment, gender discrimination, crime, and immorality, including the use of pornography."[25]

The church is recognizing the problem that pornography is creating in the lives of those in our churches, including our clergy. The church is trying to respond in the best ways it knows—by establishing rules and boundaries that may curtail the problem. The church is also using education and formal conversation in the hopes that these efforts will result in help for those already caught within the web of the addiction. The reality is that because we know the problem already exists, we must also recognize the deep shame associated with the use of pornography. With the institutional mentality that believes the sin of pornography is greater than others, the introduction and strict enforcement of these types of rules only encourages pastors who struggle with pornography to go deeper into hiding. They work to conceal, at even greater costs to themselves and their families, a behavior that is tearing apart their lives. These pastors fear the embarrassment and societal labeling they will have to face if they name their addiction and turn to their churches for help. They also fear losing their positions.

Best Practices for Self-Care

The roles of pastors and other spiritual leaders are complicated. Leaders do not know from day to day what they will face. Their hearts and minds quickly become heavy with worry, stress, pressures, demands, and the weight of human suffering and loss. The calling to serve as a minister of God is one that demands humility, grace, and wisdom. Regardless of ordination, we are called to be in community—to be the body of Christ—and to offer grace and accountability to one another in such a way as to glorify God. If those needs are not being appropriately met, the probability is that we are going to seek inappropriate ways to meet them.

As spiritual leaders, all of us are at risk of crossing boundaries, thereby violating our roles and abusing those who are vulnerable. But this risk of doing harm to those we serve or supervise can be considerably reduced through self-knowledge and self-care.

Regardless of your role in the church, it is your responsibility to aid yourself and someone else in establishing healthy and appropriate boundaries.

Be as honest with yourself as possible in answering the following questions:

- Do you really practice "honoring the Sabbath" on a weekly basis?
- In what ways do you care for your body?
    - Diet
    - Exercise
    - Sleep
    - Medical care

> Regardless of your role in the church, it is your responsibility to aid yourself and someone else in establishing healthy and appropriate boundaries.

Chapter 4: Pornography and Obscenity

- In what ways do you care for your spirit? As John Wesley would ask, "How is it with your soul?"
  - When was the last time you worshiped without being "responsible" for anything or anyone?
  - What are the spiritual disciplines you practice? How often?
- In what ways do you care for your mind?
  - How do you stimulate your mind?
  - What are you reading in your free time?
  - What occupies most of your thoughts?
- In what ways do you attend to your self (body, mind, and spirit) apart from the people and activities in your local setting of ministry?
- In what ways do you fulfill the human need for love, affection, intimacy, and affirmation?
- What is the role of the church and your family in offering accountability?
- Who really holds you accountable for your thoughts, actions, and words?
- What practices of accountability have you established regarding the following?
  - Internet sites visited
  - Text messages sent and received
  - Alone time
  - Business and vacation travel that may take you out of town and away from your family for one or more nights
- In whom do you confide and find support?
  - In whom do you confide your deepest fears?
  - With whom do you share your greatest joys?
  - What is the role of the church and your family in offering support?

As you wrestle with these questions and identify the areas on which you need to focus, seek out the help you need to be a more fulfilled and whole person. Sometimes the help you are looking for may come from within. Often it is a combination of inward work and outward guidance. Many spiritual directors, pastoral counselors, and colleagues are available to you. Consider also the role your supervisors may play in helping establish appropriate boundaries and accountability practices. There are pornography and sex addiction support groups developed especially for clergy. There are licensed psychologists, psychiatrists, and psychotherapists with specialized training in compulsive behaviors and pornographic addiction. There are those in your own community and region who have struggled in the same ways. Seek those people out and ask them to companion with you on your journey to healing and wholeness.

Notes

Chapter 5

Specialized Contexts of Ministry—FAQs

People brought babies to Jesus, hoping he might touch them. When the disciples saw it, they shooed them off. Jesus called them back. "Let these children alone. Don't get between them and me. These children are the kingdom's pride and joy. Mark this: Unless you accept God's kingdom in the simplicity of a child, you'll never get in."

—Luke 18:15-17 (The Message)

As we lead seminars and workshops on the subjects of appropriate boundaries and best practices regarding virtual communications and ministry, we receive recurring questions, especially related to vital ministries of the church that occur outside the walls of a church building. We have included some of these questions below, as well as some answers for consideration of best practices and sample language that might be helpful to you and your faith community.

Camping and Retreat Ministries

What do you think about counselors and leaders becoming "friends" through social media with campers and participants?

Review the best practices and questions for consideration that were offered in the "Social Media" section of chapter 3. There is a natural tendency to want to stay in contact with those who are meaningful and influential in your life, camping and retreat ministry leaders included. We would strongly recommend against individual "friend" connections with anyone under eighteen years of age. You can establish "group" pages, "followers," and a whole variety of more open, transparent, and safe connections than one-to-one virtual friends. Camping and retreat ministry leaders could promote this type of thinking by promoting an approved or sanctioned page, group, or account and sharing it widely and often with parents, children, and youth.

Safe Sanctuaries in a Virtual World

Best Practice

A best practice would be to include this expectation in your covenant or employment agreement with leaders and staff.

What are your thoughts about participants posting to social media while at camp or on a retreat?

Some of the blessings that might result from spontaneous, unsupervised postings include:

- great advertisement
- instant feedback to leaders about the experience
- parents knowing what is happening in the lives of their children

Some of the burdens that might result from spontaneous, unsupervised postings include:

- lack of or reduced engagement in activities, conversations, and fellowship
- a sharing of experiences and information that may take away from the experience of a camper or participant signed up to participate in a future event
- the sharing of pictures, videos, and identities of people from whom permission was not obtained
- a poor witness for Jesus Christ and the camping or retreat ministry being offered to the whole through the actions of one

Best Practices and Thoughts for Consideration

Make the camping or retreat experience a no phone/no Internet zone. Children, youth, and adults spend an inordinate amount of time online and on-screen, connecting with one another instead of being still and contemplating or experiencing God's creation without the aid of electronics. Camping and retreat ministries are such an integral part of spiritual formation, disciple making, and discovering lifelong relationships that we need to create environments in which participants can come away from the world, and often that means coming away from technology.

Consider the following:

- Make it a rule for children and youth: No electronics of any kind are allowed. If found, they will be confiscated until the retreat is over. It is also important to set expectations with your adult leaders that would be appropriate with the boundaries set for the youth.

- In some camping situations, especially with Boy Scouts and Girl Scouts, the leaders have allowed the participants to bring their phones in order to let parents know they have arrived safely. Then all the phones were collected and stored until the end of the camping trip. At that point, all the phones were redistributed so the youth could call their parents before they left the camp for their return trip home.

> Children, youth, and adults spend an inordinate amount of time online and on-screen, connecting with one another instead of being still and contemplating or experiencing God's creation without the aid of electronics.

Chapter 5: Specialized Contexts of Ministry—FAQs

- Ask adults to agree to participate fully without engagement of any kind with electronics when dealing directly with camp activities.

How do we handle cameras these days? Most of the time people use their phones, iPads, or tablets as their cameras.

One of the best ways to handle this is to be clear about the expectations and to put in writing that participants will need to make other arrangements for picture taking if they desire to have photos of the experiences and events. Here is a sample sentence that might be included in your covenant of conduct:

> *I am aware that my use of cell phones and devices used for social media is not permitted while I participate in _____. If my phone or other electronic device is also my camera, I will make other arrangements for a camera. My signature and my participation in this event signal my acceptance of this policy.*

Campus Ministries

Campus ministry is of utmost importance in the lives of young persons. They are no longer children or youth. College students are of or nearing an adult age and beginning to explore what it means to make decisions independent of parents and family, progressing toward understanding the feelings and emotions that sometimes overwhelm them, and learning how to navigate a world of mixed messages, peer pressure, and expectations that are pushing in on them from every side. They are also beginning to explore or claim for themselves the spiritual experiences and messages that have been given them throughout their childhood. Many times campus ministry becomes the avenue by which the generation that is not in our traditionalized churches is touched and transformed by the gospel of Jesus Christ. The questions asked about technology in campus ministry are often vague: "So, talk to me about how all this applies to campus ministry," or "Well, in campus ministry we are dealing with mostly people of adult age, so most of this really doesn't apply, does it?"

Here are some thoughts to consider:

- Most young people involved in college ministry are of an adult age. However, because of the power differential that is implicit in the relationship between the students and the leaders, many of the guidelines involving adults and minors need to be considered and put into practice. Read again the scenario at the beginning of chapter 3, "A Story of Power, Pain, and Technology." This story could easily be about a campus ministry leader and a student.

- Campus ministry is unique in that many times a ministry leader's level of comfort with students becomes much greater because of the communal living type of environment that college and university campuses provide. Without careful attention to boundaries and the level of sharing of personal life situations, it will be very easy for you, as a leader, to overstep boundaries and likely create a situation that is inappropriate, thereby opening the door for misconduct and sexualized behavior to occur.

> *Many times campus ministry becomes the avenue by which the generation that is not in our traditionalized churches is touched and transformed by the gospel of Jesus Christ.*

Safe Sanctuaries in a Virtual World

- It is also important to be aware of the interesting dynamic that exists in relationships between adult-age students and adult-age leaders, professors, and teachers. While the majority of states have regulations stating that it is appropriate for adults of consenting age to determine how they will interact with other adults of consenting age, the law also makes it clear that a student, while of consenting age, is not able to fully consent to engagement in any type of sexualized behavior with one who holds the greater power (e.g., a professor, leader, or teacher).

Best Practices

Best practices would include developing a covenant with your campus ministry leaders that includes expectations regarding social media and appropriate interactions with young people. The social media use policy sample forms and the youth ministry leadership covenant form found in the Sample Forms section at the end of this book, as well as a guideline for counseling, are resources that you might find helpful.

Preschool and After-school Ministries

While most of the preschool and after-school ministries can be structured to *Safe Sanctuaries* policies and procedures, many preschool and after-school ministries find themselves wrestling with two major questions:

How do we handle teachers who have personal accounts on social media, "friend" parents and/or students, and then post information that is not always in the best taste? (Some examples of posts of questionable taste include "Thanks for a great girls' night out! I am not sure how I am going to handle my loud 3rd and 4th grade class tomorrow with a hangover, though." Another post might read "FRUSTRATED . . . stay-at-home parents need to get a clue about how hard a preschool teacher works!")

Best Practices to Consider

- Develop a social media covenant that all employees must sign and adhere to as long as they are employed.

- Share with parents that you encourage social media connections between teachers and parents, and as the director, pastor, or supervisor, you practice an open-door policy for hearing parents' praises and concerns regarding their children's experiences in your ministry.

- Hold an educational workshop for older elementary and middle school students and their parents to discuss appropriate and inappropriate uses of social media and what to do when they encounter something that might make them uncomfortable.

Chapter 5: Specialized Contexts of Ministry—FAQs

We have many students who come to us after school and have homework that involves the Internet. What parameters should we put in place regarding the use of the Internet while the students are in our care?

Here are some questions and suggestions that might aid you in determining the best parameters to put in place:

- Assuming the equipment is available, either because the school provides the tablets or you have computers to use, determine what exactly needs to be accessed on the Internet—a few particular sites or general research that would involve the greater scope of the Internet.

- Consider the type of security measures you might need to put in place, including password protection for computers, controlled access to the full Internet, and controls to deny access to certain genres of sites. Who will monitor usage for appropriateness? Who will be given passwords? What guidelines will be established regarding when and for what length of time the computers or tablets can be used?

- Involve parents in the decision-making process. Have a meeting in which you ask for the parents' input about making the Internet available to their children for homework purposes, the boundaries they believe would be helpful, and the concerns they have regarding Internet usage and safety.

After gathering all this information, you are ready to make a decision. If your decision is to allow Internet usage (in whole or in part), develop a covenant that requires parental consent as well as a code of conduct for the children using the Internet. Be sure to have in writing how and when the Internet will be used, the consequences of inappropriate usage, and to whom questions should be directed.

Sports and Leisure Ministries

Many congregations host adult sports leagues, children's teams, bridge clubs, knitting groups, and a variety of other recreational activities at their churches. These sports, recreation, and leisure programs have become a major outreach ministry. Communication of all the program details, events, and schedules to the participants, parents, coaches, teachers, and leaders is a huge operation.

Here are some typical questions we've received concerning the best way to use social media with sports and leisure ministries:

What are the most practical means of communication in the context of sports and leisure ministries?

When large groups are involved, such as teams and coaches, the most practical forms of communication might be those that allow for rapid mass distribution of information. Instead of individual phone calls to each team member, a group text message would be more efficient. Instead of phone calls, you might also send an e-mail to a distribution list of the team members.

Notes

Safe Sanctuaries in a Virtual World

What information do we need to obtain from participants in the context of sports and leisure ministries?

Obtain contact information, such as phone numbers, home addresses, and e-mail addresses. You should also obtain medical information, such as a list of required medications, names of emergency contact persons, and insurance information. Parents and guardians will expect the church to treat the medical information they share with a high degree of privacy. The church needs to protect all such information to ensure that it doesn't become available for unwarranted publication, use, or gossip. There may be some variation in the information that is needed, depending on the age level of the participants in a specific activity. Ways such information could be misused are easily envisioned; therefore, plan carefully to protect the participants' and leaders' information.

Have you considered the importance of collecting a medical information and consent for treatment form from all your adult leaders? Many times we understand the importance of having these for all the players and participants, yet we forget that leaders and coaches may also become injured or require medical attention while in our care.

In the area of gathered information, it is also important to think about the general information you will have but should not share. For example, you will be able to name and identify each member of the basketball team and the senior adults travel group. But that information should not be used when posting photos on the church website or any social media outlets unless done so within guidelines that all participants have previously agreed to in writing. It is also important to communicate to parents the expectations that you as an organization hold regarding the posting of videos and photos of children and youth that are not their own.

Pastoral Moves and Social Media

Many pastors serve a lifetime in ministry and do so in a variety of different ministry settings. Social media have created and added a whole new complexity to moving, respecting the leadership of a new pastor, and recognizing and honoring the friendships you have made. The dilemma that many a pastor wrestles with today is what to do about all those "friends" on Facebook and other social media, like Twitter and Instagram, who are a part of the congregation he or she is leaving. Not to mention how "friend requests" should be handled at the next place of service.

While there are no definitive rules that dictate the ways we engage in ministry with social media, including Facebook, and our participation in the itinerant system, there are some questions to consider as we create healthy boundaries for ending a time of service in one place in order to make ourselves fully available and present in a new ministry setting.

Will you go where you are sent . . .

Wherever you go, it is because the bishop, the cabinet, and, hopefully, the power of the Holy Spirit have seen it right and appropriate to appoint you to this new place of service. How will you engage fully, in body, mind, and spirit, in the ministries of this

Chapter 5: Specialized Contexts of Ministry—FAQs

place and community even as you use Facebook? Consider these additional questions as you prepare to go forward in ministry:

- *What information is on your Facebook page? What message does this send to those who might be signing on to "check out" their new pastor?*

- *For what purpose will you use Facebook in this new setting?*

- *Will you solicit any "friends" from your new congregation that are on Facebook?*

- *Will you accept a request from any person who invites you to be their friend?*

- *How will you handle friend requests from children and youth in your congregation?*

- *Do you have a reason not to accept any friend requests from people in your new congregation?*

Consider having a conversation with your new Pastor/Staff-Parish Relations Committee (P/SPRC) regarding your use of Facebook and the parameters you have set up for yourself in this place of ministry. This would also be a good time to learn if there is a church Facebook page, identify the administrator(s) of the page, and review the guidelines that have been developed regarding updates, security, postings, and so on.

. . . and stay away from where you have been?

Once upon a time this question was easily handled because of the number of miles between one place and another and the cost of long-distance phone service. In this day and age of unlimited talk and social media, staying away from where you have been is a bit trickier. Here are some options to aid you in answering yes to this question:

- Consider changing your cell number to a local number in your new place of service.

- Write an e-mail or a newsletter article to the entire congregation, letting them know of your new appointment, and what this means in terms of relationships as "their pastor" in the days, months, and years to come.

- Have face-to-face conversations with church members and friends within the congregation who you know are going to have a hard time with your moving. The conversation should focus on your pastoral authority and its shift to the new pastor who is coming to their church.

- Have a conversation with the pastor who is following you to establish boundaries regarding pastoral visits, e-mails, social media engagement, funerals, weddings, and so on. Share these boundaries with the SPRC so that all are duly informed and can serve one another as an accountability system.

- After you move, consider paring down your "friends" list, removing church members from your previous congregation who "followed" you because you were their pastor.

- Be clear and consistent with those who remain "friends" from a previous appointment that you are their friend, not their pastor. Continue to encourage them to turn to their new pastor every time a pastoral need or concern

Notes

arises. Seek permission from the new pastor who is currently appointed in that location before participating in a funeral, conducting a wedding, or engaging in any pastoral care toward members of a congregation to which you are no longer appointed.

How can you do this without hurting people's feelings or seeming to be rude?

Remind yourself that you are trying to live out John Wesley's Rules and model them for God's people:

1. Do no harm.
2. Do good.
3. Stay in love with God.

Develop each conversation within the framework of your denomination, or in this case our United Methodist connectional system. Keep the following points in mind:

- We are itinerant.
- We have covenanted to go where we are sent. It is a part of our ordination/licensing.
- We seek to honor and encourage the ministry of those who come next to lead this congregation. It is not our desire to serve as an obstacle or stumbling block to the next leadership.
- This is an exercise in Christian living—it is about loving one another, as well as holding one another accountable in Christian love.
- Boundary setting and boundary keeping are steps toward self-care as well as care for God's people. As the pastor/shepherd of a congregation, we are called to provide consistent and predictable behavior that is in keeping with our being faithful witnesses of Jesus Christ.

Are there other things you need to consider as you reflect on your use of Facebook and other social media and your role as a leader in The United Methodist Church?

- Consider the reasons why you have social media accounts, personal and professional. What content is available on your page? What security measures are in place to limit the scope of material that is accessible to the general public?
- Consider what you post (links, status updates, pictures, videos, etc.). How does this reflect on your role and identity as a leader in The United Methodist Church?
- Remember that unlike a blog, e-mail, or website, once something is posted on social media, even if removed, it is often still available for others to view and retrieve.
- Be cautious of your use of language, exaggeration, opinions shared, copyrighted material, and photos of others.

Chapter 5: Specialized Contexts of Ministry—FAQs

- Refrain from sharing speculation, sensitive information, obscene or pornographic materials, and derogatory comments regarding individuals, groups, and The United Methodist Church.

Visitor and New Member Assimilation

Every church hopes to have visitors. Every church hopes the visitors will enjoy their experience in the church enough to return again and become members of the congregation. The church I (Joy) attend devotes careful planning to its hospitality ministries for visitors. We also plan carefully for helping our new members find ways to become involved and engaged with the ministries of the congregation in order to build strong connections with members.

When you visit my church for worship the first time, you will be welcomed by our greeters—at every door. When you enter the sanctuary or fellowship hall for worship, or a classroom for Sunday school, you'll be invited to sign the Welcome Notes—a pad designed to allow members and visitors to give name, address, phone, and e-mail information, as well as to request a contact from the church or more information about the church. The information you give to us on the Welcome Notes will be collected, and by Monday morning, the church staff members will have it on their desks. Requests for contacts and additional information are responded to right away. First-time visitors who provide e-mail or phone contact information receive messages or calls from one of the ministers. Following your next visit, you will receive any additional information you may have requested and a friendly call or message from a church member. Following your third visit, if you've given us your address, you'll be warmly welcomed by one of our members as he or she delivers a batch of homemade cookies right to your door.

What is planned for the new members of your church? In my church, there is an assimilation committee that plans ways to help the new members feel included, welcomed, and encouraged to participate in a variety of settings beyond worship services. Every event or project requires specifically targeted communication among the planners, members, and new members. Obviously, our success depends on the effectiveness of all our communications. We must use communication channels that will support our goal of encouraging the new members to participate in our ministries and become better acquainted with the congregation.

When thinking about how to communicate with visitors and new members, the need for getting messages out must be balanced with the need for protecting the privacy of visitors' and members' contact information. Consider how personalized and individualized each communication needs to be and how widely to share information: Will an announcement be put in the worship bulletin, on the church website, or in the printed newsletter? Will an announcement be sent by phone, e-mail, text message, or US mail? Give careful attention to answering these questions to better assure that your church is a safe sanctuary in the virtual world for members and visitors.

Notes

Chapter 6

Training and Response

> I'm single-minded in pursuit of you; don't let me miss the road signs you've posted. I've banked your promises in the vault of my heart so I won't sin myself bankrupt. Be blessed, GOD; train me in your ways of wise living.
> —Psalm 119:10-12 (THE MESSAGE)

A full and comprehensive strategy of education, protection, and prevention of misconduct, in person or through the use of any type of multimedia format in your local church, cannot be successfully implemented without a substantial amount of time and energy being expended before any training takes place. The training that is offered to leaders needs to be thoughtful, well-informed, worshipful, and practical. While there is not any one particular way that training should be conducted, it is imperative that training occur at least annually in order that current trends, new understandings, and the current needs of your congregation and community are being addressed. The following model is designed to be used with your church's leaders, both volunteer and employed, who have any part in communication, leadership, relationship building or nurturing, or interfacing responsibilities with the community and larger world. This model, which can be easily modified to use with other groups as needed, is designed as a two- to three-hour workshop. Many churches are also utilizing training tools such as DVDs, PowerPoint presentations, and their websites to make training sessions more easily accessible. Some helpful resources are listed in the Sources and Resources section of this book.

Opening Worship

Opening Prayer

Gracious God, we have heard the call of your Spirit and remember the passion we had at the beginning of our journey with you. We are grateful for who you are and take great delight in your commandments. Given great responsibility like Adam and Eve, we too resist boundaries and prohibitions. So God, let your Spirit awaken and renew us this day, so that we might again have delight in your commandments and walk

Safe Sanctuaries in a Virtual World

humbly with you. Bless our time together, letting our hearts, minds, and spirits commune with your Spirit. We ask this prayer in the name and strength of Jesus Christ, our Lord, your Son, our Savior. Amen.

Suggested Scriptures

Psalm 119:10-16

Ephesians 4:1-16

James 2:2-10

1 Corinthians 12

Brief Devotion

Begin with any of these scriptures, or some of your own choosing. Describe how the scripture reveals the value and blessings of caring for one another in all of life. Acknowledge the ways your congregation lives out the gospel's call to care for one another. Conclude your devotion with the introduction of the virtual world boundaries and best practices as a strategy to continue to address the ways your congregation is going to care well for one another and the community.

Introductory Information

Current Occurrences

Set the stage for the substance of the event by introducing recent news reports from your own community's newspapers or television broadcasts related to incidents of harm and sexual misconduct that have occurred through the use of online media and technology. You could also present the news material related to any current litigation involving churches or other institutions and claims of misconduct that involve Facebook, cyberbullying, online pornography, and the like.

Current Statistics

Invite the participants to share with one another the ways technology is used in their daily lives, and the ways they see it as a positive benefit for church use. Quote the statistical information from this resource or from other sources available to you. Provide this information as a handout for the participants or as part of a slide presentation so that the students have it in front of them for reference.

A full and comprehensive strategy of education, protection, and prevention of misconduct, in person or through the use of any type of multimedia format in your local church, cannot be successfully implemented without a substantial amount of time and energy being expended before any training takes place. The training that is offered to leaders needs to be thoughtful, well-informed, worshipful, and practical.

Chapter 6: Training and Response

Reasons to Implement Virtual World Boundaries and Best Practices

- Our church's witness is extended into the community and the world through the use of social media and the Internet. As a community of faith that offers a safe haven and sanctuary for all who seek advice, help, and nurture, it is important that our online witness match our Sunday morning witness.

- Our church is a place where more than just facts of abuse and harm related to the World Wide Web are taught. We also teach and proclaim our faith values of integrity, compassion, justice, repentance, and grace through the ways we care for and respond to acts of misconduct, harm, and abuse.

- We desire our church to be a place where children, youth, and adults can come and develop deepened spiritual resources and faith, and remain connected to one another beyond the walls of the building. The ways in which we invite others to be a part of the community and the ways we treat one another and engage in the virtual world will greatly affect how community is established and nurtured in the church.

- Our church wants all persons to learn how to respond to painful and confusing events of life using the wisdom of the scriptures and the strength of fellowship with other believers. A part of this strength of community is the integrity with which we love one another even as we love ourselves.

Blessings and Burdens of Multimedia Communications and Communities

Use the information found in the subsequent pages to help people understand the burdens and blessings of:

- instant access to the Internet and its resources
- social media
- cell phones
- blogs, e-mails, and web pages

Power and Vulnerability

Lead a discussion of the concepts of power and vulnerability and how these can lead to harm and abuse in the church. Use some of the scenarios found in prior chapters or the news reports you shared earlier to illustrate the balance-of-power concept. In each illustration, have the participants list the sources of power available to the one causing harm. Then have the participants identify the specific factors and circumstances that made the victim vulnerable. If time permits, you might consider using a video segment here to illustrate the concepts you have just addressed. The resource list in the Sources and Resources section provides some appropriate sources for reflection and review.

Notes

What Are We Doing to Ensure Safety and Community?

Present the new policies and procedures for implementing the Internet, and its information, resources, and social media in the church's ministries. Give participants time to read the policies and allow time for questions and discussion as you review each section with the group.

Invite participants to sign the conduct policies in covenantal agreement as they serve as leaders in your church's ministry.

Summarize

These reports and data demonstrate that we cannot ignore the possibility that harm and abuse might happen in any area of ministry of our faith community. For the sake of Jesus Christ and for the protection of all God's children, we need to intentionally work to prevent misconduct, abuse, and harm from occurring.

Closing Worship

Return to the scripture reading from the opening worship moments. Read aloud Ephesians 4:1-16.

Invite the participants to share aloud how the body of Christ is made more full through our engagement of technology.

Ask the participants to pray responsively with you by saying after each sentence prayer, "Unite our hearts with your Spirit!"

> Leader: O God, by our presence here today, we come boldly asking,
>
> **People:** Unite our hearts with your Spirit!
>
> Leader: We desire to be your disciples, to teach in your name, to love with your heart, to speak with your words,
>
> **People:** Unite our hearts with your Spirit!
>
> Leader: Help us that we might love mercy, seek justice, and always walk humbly with you.
>
> **People:** Unite our hearts with your Spirit!
>
> Leader: May our interactions with one another, whether face-to-face, computer to computer, or iPhone to tablet, bring you honor and lead people to you.
>
> **People:** Unite our hearts with your Spirit!

Chapter 6: Training and Response

Leader: We commit ourselves, and all the technology that we might use, to you, to serve as a light to the nations and a glimmer of hope in a dark and hurting world.

People: Unite our hearts with your Spirit!

Leader: Gracious God, thank you for the incredible gifts you have created and gathered together in this room. Thank you for their commitment to you and to your people. Guide us all, O God, in creating healthy relationships that meet our needs for love and affirmation. Having cared for ourselves, guide us as we seek to provide the sacred space for your people in need, space where their shadows can come into your light and be redeemed. We pray in the name of Jesus Christ, our Rock and our Redeemer. Amen.

Offering

Ask the participants to bring forward their signed covenant forms as a sign of offering themselves in ministry and leadership. Sing the Doxology.

Benediction

May the grace of the Lord Jesus Christ, the love of God, and the power of the Holy Spirit guide and direct you and all you do. Amen.

A Model for Response

This resource is designed to assist congregations in preparing response plans for any ethical violations, abuse, or immoral behavior that affects the faith community. This section is focused on what it means for us to make a faithful response to the victims of abuse and harm.

When a child, youth, or adult is harmed within the safety of a community of faith, there are many victims in addition to the one who has been physically or emotionally harmed. All of the victims are in need of healing ministry. Who are the other victims?

Victims may include any of the following:

- family members of the child, youth, or vulnerable adult who was harmed
- peers of the child, youth, or vulnerable adult who was harmed
- the staff and volunteer workers in the church's ministry
- the congregation as a community of faith
- the family of the accused perpetrator of the abuse

Each victim, or group of victims, will need to be included in our responsive ministry.

The harming of children, youth, and adults within the church or outside the church is not a new occurrence. It has certainly existed for longer than we want to admit.

> When a child, youth, or adult is harmed within the safety of a community of faith, there are many victims in addition to the one who has been physically or emotionally harmed. All of the victims are in need of healing ministry.

We have begun to realize that the injury inflicted on individuals is multiplied exponentially when it is kept secret or denied within the congregation. Hidden abuses continue to cause anger, confusion, and fear in the congregation for years to come.

Revisiting "A Story of Power, Pain, and Technology"

Review the story of Grace Church and Reverend Jones, Sally, and Reverend Thomas in chapter 3. It is easy to see how this church's failure to address the issues of anger, fear, confusion, and grief following the report of abuse had devastating and long-lasting consequences for everyone.

When the integrity of a church's pastor and other leaders is seriously questioned, and when the congregation begins to divide into factions, intentional effort will certainly be required to repair the harm and restore the community of faith to wholeness and unity.

How can your church be in ministry to any and all victims of abuse and harm? Ministry after abuse has occurred must be aimed at finding justice for all and healing for those who are suffering. Justice is seldom achieved in a short time, and healing usually comes slowly. Thus patience will be a key factor in responsive ministry. Think about the length of time your congregation has spent developing its abuse-prevention policies and procedures for children, youth, and vulnerable adults. If you worked on this for a year or more, you learned how complex this endeavor can be. Achieving healing and justice after abuse is also complex and will take time. The congregation won't be able to simply sponsor one workshop, provide a video to watch, or listen to a sermon series on justice and forgiveness and expect to successfully create enough understanding for healing to be realized.

Response ministry with victims, both the individual and the congregation, is very similar to ministry with those going through a grief process. When you begin to realize that ministry to victims of abuse and harm is a process, not simply a onetime event, you will be better able to understand the measure of time and devotion that may be needed for the victims and the congregation to be restored to a renewed state of wholeness and faith. Full-response ministry can be offered through the efforts of a team of leaders working as a response team. The response team could include congregational leaders, counselors, and community resource persons. The composition of the response team will be guided by the facts of the situation that is being addressed.

First Things First

Truth-telling will be your first step in a healing and restorative ministry. Honest communication about the facts of what happened must occur. Truth-telling never includes gossip or speculation or embellishment of the facts. Truth-telling never allows for blaming the victim!

Let's think about how your ministry leaders will engage in the honest communication necessary for truth-telling.

Begin by following the procedures you have in place for reporting an incident of abuse to law enforcement authorities and denominational officials. If you are reporting an

Chapter 6: Training and Response

incident of physical abuse, emotional abuse, sexual abuse, or neglect, you will make the report to the local law enforcement authorities or to the state office of adult protective services. If a report of theft, fraud, sexual exploitation, or another crime needs to be made, then you will contact the local law enforcement authorities. It is also important to make sure your designated church media spokesperson is notified and made aware of the factual information, so any media questions can be responded to in appropriate ways. In the scenario we reviewed above, the report was appropriately made both to local law enforcement authorities and to the senior pastor of the church.

By the time you have completed this initial report, it is quite possible that rumors will be spreading among the members of the congregation about the incident or allegations. At this time, it is important to provide honest and only factual information. This may begin with a letter to the members that briefly explains the incident and the initial action taken by the church. The letter should not include the identification of the individual victim or the identification of the accused perpetrators. However, the letter should include a statement of the actions taken to ensure the safety of all in the church and to assure the continued delivery of ministry to the congregation.

Think again of the hypothetical situation reviewed above. List three items or thoughts you think it would be important to include in the letter written to the congregation:

1.

2.

3.

Some factual information to consider including in the letter would be: (1) the date and type of allegation; (2) the names of authorities and supervisory personnel who are aware of the situation (law enforcement, church staff, bishop, district superintendent, etc.); (3) the actions taken to date; (4) the date and place of any planned congregational meeting regarding the allegations; and (5) where and to whom questions can be directed.

A Congregational Meeting

Experienced members of response teams know that it is helpful to announce in the letter to the congregation members that a congregational meeting has been scheduled for a certain time and place and all are invited to attend. A congregational meeting often proves to be a powerful aspect of the ministry of truth-telling and, eventually, healing. Planning for such a meeting must be done carefully and intentionally if it is to be a time in which clarity can be achieved. It is not good planning for a response team member to ask to have a moment in the Sunday worship announcement time and say, "I know you've probably heard by now that one of our members was abused this week. I'd like for everyone to pray for her. If you have any questions, just let me know." An off-the-cuff and startling speech such as this will be harmful and not truly responsive to the situation. If an invitation is given to open the floor for discussion in the worship service, you may be creating a most uncomfortable situation for some who are present and who would not want to be included in such a discussion. This open invitation can shock members who have heard no previous reports or rumors. This type of open invitation also may cause members who themselves have been

Notes

victims of abuse to suddenly remember those past traumatic events and thus experience strongly negative emotions. Needless to say, this type of approach to the congregational meeting could be perceived by the victim's family as highly insulting. If it appears that their loved one's injury is being treated as nothing more than a moment in the Sunday morning announcements, the result will surely be hurt feelings and anger. Don't take such an impulsive and disorganized approach to a congregational meeting! In litigation that might develop, such an approach could be characterized by some as an uncaring attitude from the church leadership.

You must plan carefully for this first congregational meeting. Give everyone advance notice of the date, time, and meeting location. Select the meeting leaders very carefully. It is important for the pastor to be one of the leaders, unless, of course, the pastor is the accused abuser. In that case, the pastor most certainly will not be a leader of any congregational meeting regarding this matter. It is helpful to seek the advice and leadership of denominational representatives if you are part of a connectional system. Also, in this meeting and subsequent meetings, it is important that lay leaders be present. The lay leaders must come prepared to provide information about the actions taken by the church thus far in response to the abuse or allegations of abuse. The denominational representative may not have to do or say anything specific except to reinforce the support from the denomination as the church deals with this crisis. This may seem like a minimal role and contribution to make, but it must not be undervalued. The presence of a denominational leader who is supportive of the church's efforts to address this crisis will be much appreciated by the leaders and by the congregation.

Finally, it is important to include a qualified counselor in the leadership team for the congregational meetings. It is also sometimes more helpful if the counselor is not a member of the congregation. This meeting will bring forth strong feelings and emotions. By having a counselor present, the leadership team is able to offer help immediately to those who experience strong feelings, rather than putting off or minimizing the feelings. We are convinced that it would be virtually impossible to find a congregation today that does not include survivors of abuse of some kind. It is highly likely that any survivors of abuse will have strong reactions to the facts of the current incident of abuse and unethical behavior. A counselor's presence can be helpful for those persons as well as for others.

A number of United Methodist annual conferences have formed response teams for the purpose of assisting local congregations in responding to allegations or incidents of abuse and harm. Response teams also exist in other denominations. If your annual conference has a response team in place, consult with the team leader as you plan the congregational meeting. The response team can assist you with planning, be present for the meeting, and possibly provide one or more counselors for the meeting. More complete information regarding response teams is available from the General Commission on the Status and Role of Women at www.gcsrw.org, your annual conference's staff, or from my office at joy@safesanctuariesconsulting.com.

Let's go back once again to the hypothetical situation at Grace Church involving Reverend Jones, Sally, and Reverend Thomas. As a leader planning the first congregational meeting following this crisis, what details would you plan for in advance?

Chapter 6: Training and Response

1.

2.

3.

What resources would you gather in advance for the meeting?

1.

2.

3.

The Meeting Agenda: What should happen in a congregational meeting following an incident of harm or abuse? You will need to include time on the agenda for the following:

- Fact sharing
- Small-group conversation and sharing time
- Closing moments of reflection and worship
- Acknowledgment of counselors and other resources available

Begin with fact sharing. Open this section of the agenda by giving an accurate description of what has happened and what actions have been taken or will be taken. Answer questions as fully as possible without jeopardizing any ongoing investigation by the church or local law enforcement agencies. Protect the identity of the victim to give the family as much privacy as possible. Don't hesitate to answer questions by saying, "We don't know the answer to that yet." It is better to admit not knowing the answer than to speculate about the situation or the outcome of an ongoing investigation.

Divide the attendees into small groups of five or six persons for the small-group conversation time. Have a facilitator available for each small group. If you have a response team in your denomination, the team may be able to provide facilitators for you, or they may be able to suggest qualified persons from your local community. The small-group facilitator should begin by letting the members know that it is permissible to express *any* emotion within the small group. All those in the group will be allowed time to share, and there will be no debate or argument about the validity of feelings and emotions that are expressed. The purpose of the small-group conversation segment of the meeting agenda is to help people verbalize their feelings about the incident. The purpose is *not* to develop a strategy or to elicit premature forgiveness for the perpetrator of the abuse. This part of the meeting may take about an hour and may be the longest part of the meeting.

When you see that the small groups are bringing their time together to a close, reassemble the entire group. Acknowledge the realities of this situation and offer a prayer for the congregation as it works to achieve justice for all and healing for all those who are suffering.

What would you include in a closing time of worship and devotion?

1.

2.

3.

Notes

List three reasons why it is important to include these particular elements of worship at this time in the congregation's life:

1.

2.

3.

Some possible resources for worship to be used during this time can be found in the Sources and Resources section of this book.

Continuing Ministry of Response

Restoration of the victim and the church to spiritual health and wholeness will be a process that takes quite some time. The letter to the congregation and the congregational meeting discussed above are not all a church needs to return to spiritual health. However, you can use the feelings, fears, and needs expressed in the first congregational meeting to develop a plan for a continuing response to the victims—the individuals and the congregation. The response team, other existing groups within the church, a newly created group, or a combination of these can be used to attend to this ongoing ministry of healing, justice, education, counseling, and worship. Each church will have its own approach to the continuing ministry of response. The important thing is that it does actually continue.

Educational ministries may include programs covering topics such as:

- the consequences of abuse and harm—physical, emotional, psychological, and spiritual
- the importance of church security protocols in every aspect of communication
- ways to protect children, youth, and adults from exploitation and abuse through cyber communications such as social media
- resources in your community offering legal assistance for victims of cyber crimes such as sexting, fraud, and identity theft
- resources in your community offering help and guidance in handling addictions to pornography, gambling, sex, drugs, and alcohol
- Bible study and theological study of the concepts of justice, mercy, repentance, forgiveness, reconciliation, and healing

Programs might also include speakers with expertise in any of these areas. Current information is available from many of the resources listed in the Sources and Resources section of this book. Your state and local law enforcement agencies can provide helpful information. Use Sunday school classes, fellowship dinner meetings, study groups, and other settings to present such programs. Give advance notice and publicity about each program. Let's look again at "A Story of Power, Pain, and Technology." What would your team of leaders choose as the first educational programs to be created following the events in this situation?

Chapter 6: Training and Response

1.

2.

3.

Possible programs include the following:

- Discussion of parenting teens and young adults in a digital age. This would be an introductory workshop to share with parents the ways common technology is being used by younger generations and safety measures they might consider putting in place.

- A coffeehouse conversation for teens regarding their rights to personal safety in the digital world as part of a faith community and youth/young adult ministries.

- A program with your Staff-Parish Relations Committee or equivalent personnel committee to consider ways to set up an appropriate system of checks and balances regarding electronic media.

What settings would you choose for the educational programs?

1.

2.

3.

The continuing ministry of response may need to include counseling or support groups. Families suffering as a result of the abuse of a family member could benefit from such supportive services. Locate qualified leaders within your congregation or your community. Enlist their assistance in the formation of support groups. Plan thoroughly and carefully for support group leadership.

Individual counseling services will be of great value in your congregation's efforts to assist the healing of victims and church members following an incident of harm or abuse. There are costs involved in creating counseling ministries. You may be able to make the necessary financial arrangements with a trained and experienced counselor so that the victim and the victim's family receive sufficient counseling to achieve healing without any monetary cost to them. It might be feasible for your church to collaborate with neighboring churches to create a counseling center available to members of all the congregations as well as the community. This type of service would also be valuable to the family members of the accused perpetrator of abuse. We cannot condone in any way the behavior of an alleged perpetrator; however, it is appropriate to recognize that in this situation the extended family members of the accused perpetrator may be suffering terribly. Offering counseling to them as an act of grace and healing does not condone the unethical or abusive behavior.

All continuing ministries of response are founded on the idea that providing opportunities for openness and honesty leads to healing recovery. We have learned that there is no benefit to offering premature forgiveness to the perpetrator. For healing to occur, it is necessary that painful consequences be endured, not only by the victim, who suffered first, but also by the perpetrator of the harm and abuse. When the perpetrator of

> Restoration of the victim and the church to spiritual health and wholeness will be a process that takes quite some time.

abuse is able to demonstrate real sorrow and repentance, then it will be reasonable for the congregation to offer the grace of forgiveness. The victim may or may not be able to forgive the harm suffered, and no pressure to offer forgiveness should be brought by the church leaders on the victim for the sake of making the members of the church or the perpetrator feel better. In the case of any form of sexual abuse, whether it occurs as a cyber crime or a physical crime, we must be clear that when the church is approached by a convicted sex offender seeking involvement in the ministry, offering something called "forgiveness" to the offender without expecting full accountability from him or her is seriously ill-advised for the church. Offering premature forgiveness or reconciliation does not assist the offender in changing his or her behavior and will be deeply hurtful to the victim in the congregation.

Finally, the leaders of the response team or other groups who have guided the continuing ministries of response may decide to offer another time for sharing to the whole congregation. Use this time to assess how much healing and recovery has taken place up to this point. Review the new steps, procedures, and training that have been implemented to reduce the likelihood that abuse will occur again. Identify any remaining needs or issues that have not been resolved and possible ways to address them. Regular follow-up with the participants in the congregational meeting could also be a part of your responsive ministries. Find a time to offer a worship experience where persons can offer expressions of gratitude for the progress being made toward healing and for renewal of the congregation's commitment to doing justice. Worship will also afford the group a chance to offer prayers for the work of building all the processes needed for the church to be the safe sanctuary it is called to be.

Let's look again at this situation we have been examining. Review the possible forms of continuing response after abuse or harm.

1.

2.

3.

Make a list of the costs and expenses that a church would incur to develop these ministries:

1.

2.

3.

4.

Usually the largest cost is for the time given and devoted to the responsive ministries by the staff and volunteers.

Make a list of the benefits a church would receive as a result of these ministries:

1.

2.

Chapter 6: Training and Response

    3.

    4.

Some of the benefits might include: (1) building and maintaining the positive reputation of the church in the community; (2) being recognized for your willingness to reach out to and embrace the hurting and the broken; and (3) healing within the congregation that occurs in individuals' lives because of past trauma, harm, or abuse they have suffered.

Has your congregation experienced a time when a child, youth, or vulnerable adult was harmed by abusive communications in cyberspace and sought help from the church? If so, what responses were made?

    1.

    2.

    3.

What were the costs of each program or type of response made by the congregation?

    1.

    2.

    3.

What were the benefits of each program or type of response made by the congregation?

    1.

    2.

    3.

Some of the benefits might include: (1) education for the greater community; (2) healing of trauma (emotional and spiritual) for the victim and the congregation; (3) restoration of integrity of leadership; (4) a realized embodiment of Christ's love, repentance, forgiveness, and healing that is felt, experienced, and preached; and (5) a reduced possibility of something of this nature occurring again in this faith community.

When an allegation of abuse or harm occurs in our communities of faith, we have the responsibility to fully and faithfully embody Christ's love, grace, and accountability. The grace of God is equally yoked with Christ's understanding of the accountability we have with one another in the covenant of community.

Reaction or Response?

In every situation of harm or abuse, alleged or substantiated, we are faced with one question that makes all the difference: Will we react or respond?

A reaction is a knee-jerk, emotionally laden pathway that is founded in fear, anger, disbelief, and a lack of preparation. Response is a thoughtful, prepared pathway that is rooted in love, justice, and healing.

> In every situation of harm or abuse, alleged or substantiated, we are faced with one question that makes all the difference: Will we react or respond?

Safe Sanctuaries in a Virtual World

As a people of God, we are called to love mercy, seek justice, and walk humbly with God (Micah 6:8). This requires more than a knee-jerk reaction. Our response to God is responsible planning so that when an allegation occurs we can appropriately respond with love, mercy, grace, compassion, and justice to all who are broken and harmed.

Notes

Sample Forms

Sample Social Media Use Policy for Employees

Social networking is quickly becoming integrated into everyday life. Electronic tools aid us in communication, relationships, and information sharing in ways that were never before conceived as possible. The use of social media and networking often also causes lines to blur between work, personal life, and church relationships. In general, what you do in your personal time is a personal decision. However, activities during or outside of work that are shared via social media may have adverse effects on your job performance, leadership ability, and witness of Jesus Christ, and need to be considered carefully. By simply identifying yourself as an employee of [church name], either directly or as a part of your user profile, you are creating perceptions about what it means to be a part of [church name].

As such, this policy is offered to provide official guidelines for social media use for all employees of [church name]. It is the expectation that all who participate in social media use will understand and follow these guidelines.

As a child of God, a member of the church universal, and as an employee of [church name], I covenant and agree to use Facebook and other similar social media in ways that bring honor to God and show respect for self and for all others who might view my posts.

In particular, I covenant to (initial in the space provided after you have read and agreed to each bulleted item):

- Recognize and respect that my behaviors and actions online are also a reflection of how other Christians and people associated with [church name] may be portrayed. _____

- Recognize that all my posted words, images, and links are reflections on me individually, as a disciple of Jesus Christ, and as an employee of [church name]. Recognizing this, I will refrain from posting anything regarding inappropriate conduct, such as drug or alcohol use or any item that contains profanity, degrading humor of any kind, ethnic or racial slurs, personal insults, obscenity, vulgarity, nudity, or pornography. _____

- Obey the laws governing defamation, discrimination, harassment, and copyright and fair use of proprietary or confidential information. _____

- Work within my assigned ministry to establish appropriate boundaries especially as related to building relationships online with children, youth, parents, and other constituents of [church name]. _____

- Be very careful not to be a hindrance or cause harm to the staff, pastors, members, or ministries of [church name]. _____

- Speak respectfully in my online posts and communications of and to all persons; and I will refrain from negative or disrespectful posts as well as posts on objectionable or inflammatory topics. _____

- Respect confidentiality and personal privacy. In the event I receive confidential or private information regarding a person or family involved in [church name], I will not disseminate that information without receiving direct express consent and permission to do so. _____

- Respect differences, appreciate diversity of opinions, and speak and conduct myself in a professional and ethical manner at all times. _____

- Remember that everything I post online is discoverable and can be seen and shared for a very long time. _____

- Seek advice from my ministry team leader before posting anything if I have even a small doubt about the reasonableness of the post. _____

- Regularly monitor the amount of time I spend on social media, the ways in which I am utilizing social media, and its effects on my ministry and service in Christ's name. _____

Signed: _____ (Employee)

Date: _____

(Each item above is to be initialed by the employee. The signed and dated document will be retained in the employee's record.)

Sample Social Media Use Policy for Volunteers

Social networking is quickly becoming integrated into everyday life. Electronic tools aid us in communication, relationships, and information sharing in ways that were never before conceived as possible. The use of social media and networking often also causes lines to blur between work, personal life, and church relationships. In general, what you do in your personal time is a personal decision. However, activities during or outside of volunteer work that are shared via social media may have adverse effects on your job performance, leadership ability, and witness of Jesus Christ and need to be considered carefully. By simply identifying yourself as a volunteer of [church name], either directly or as a part of your user profile, you are creating perceptions about what it means to be a part of [church name].

As such, this policy is offered to provide official guidelines for social media use for all volunteers of [church name]. It is the expectation that all who participate in social media use will understand and follow these guidelines.

As a child of God, a member of the church universal, and as a volunteer of [church name], I covenant and agree to use Facebook and other similar social media in ways that bring honor to God and show respect for self and for all others who might view my posts.

In particular, I covenant to (initial in the space provided after you have read and agreed to each bulleted item):

- recognize and respect that my behaviors and actions online are also a reflection of how other Christians and people associated with [church name] may be portrayed. _____

- recognize that all my posted words, images, and links are reflections on me individually, as a disciple of Jesus Christ, and as a volunteer of [church name]. Recognizing this, I will refrain from posting anything regarding inappropriate conduct such as drug or alcohol use or any item that contains profanity, degrading humor of any kind, ethnic or racial slurs, personal insults, obscenity, vulgarity, nudity, or pornography. _____

- obey the laws governing defamation, discrimination, harassment, and copyright and fair use of proprietary or confidential information. _____

- work within my assigned ministry to establish appropriate boundaries especially as related to building relationships online with children, youth, parents, and other constituents of [church name]. _____

- be very careful not to be a hindrance or cause harm to the staff, pastors, members, or ministries of [church name]. _____

- speak respectfully in my online posts and communications of and to all persons; and I will refrain from negative or disrespectful posts as well as posts on objectionable or inflammatory topics. _____

- respect confidentiality and personal privacy. In the event I receive confidential or private information regarding a person or family involved at [church name], I will not disseminate that information without receiving direct, express consent and permission to do so. _____

- respect differences, appreciate diversity of opinions, and speak and conduct myself in a faithful and ethical manner at all times. _____

- remember that everything I post online is discoverable and can be seen and shared for a very long time. _____

- seek advice from my ministry team leader before posting anything if I have even a small doubt about the reasonableness of the post. _____

- regularly monitor the amount of time I spend on social media, the ways in which I am utilizing social media, and its effects on my volunteer ministry and service in Christ's name. _____

Signed: _____ (Volunteer)

Date: _____

(Each item above is to be initialed by the volunteer. The signed and dated document will be retained in the volunteer's record.)

Sample Youth Ministry Leadership Covenant

As a leader in youth ministry, you are called to exhibit the highest of Christian values and serve in ways that honor Christ. Students in your care and charge are seeking and searching. They are hungry to discover even more fully what it means to be a Christ-follower. Your examples of servant leadership, compassion, kindness, forgiveness, self-control, patience, and love will serve as signposts throughout their journey.

This covenant is created to encourage your God-giftedness, your unique talents, and your leadership, while also helping you to establish and maintain appropriate and healthy relationships with the youth of our community.

Teamwork always takes precedence over individualism. The goal is community for everyone involved.

You can nurture disciples only as much as you offer yourself as a disciple. Gifted leaders have a passion for God and a desire to share God's love.

Youth will seek you out for advice, personal sharing, and direction. It is important that you respect the confidentiality with which something is shared, unless you are required by law to share information you have been given.

It is the expectation that as a leader, your life will reflect a high level of personal and moral integrity.

While it is not prohibited for youth leaders to date one another, it does create an interesting dynamic, especially when a breakup occurs. If you date another youth leader, you are asked to use discretion and Christlike judgment. It is absolutely prohibited for a youth leader to date or engage in any sexualized behavior with a youth. Sexual misconduct of any type will not be tolerated.

All of us face situations of fear, frustration, and loss in our lives. You are asked to refrain from sharing with youth information pertaining to your personal life issues. You are also asked to use careful and judicious judgment in sharing any past experiences of poor judgment or behavior as a teaching tool.

While it is most appropriate to be friendly to youth at youth group, in the community, and in the church, it is not appropriate to begin a friendship with youth that will spill over into fraternization outside of sponsored youth activities. Again, it is expressly prohibited for youth leaders to date youth. Maintaining appropriate boundaries with youth is an acknowledgment of the power differential that is implicit in your role as a leader. These boundaries will help you gain their respect and will enhance your ability and effectiveness in disciplining or counseling them.

As a child of God, a member of the church universal, and as an employee of [church name], I covenant and agree to (initial in the space provided after you have read and agreed to each bulleted item):

- not abuse alcohol or drugs in any inappropriate or illegal manner, engage in sexual immorality, or participate in the sharing of music that contains language or messages that others may find offensive. _____

- work as a team and submit myself and my will to the assigned leader of any particular mission, event or activity. _____

- attend to my own spiritual growth through prayer, Bible study, worship, and participation in the community of faith. _____

- display exemplary moral character and integrity through my participation in online social media, the appropriate use of my cell phone and other mobile devices, and my engagement with others utilizing these devices. I will abstain from and encourage youth to abstain from sexting, cyberbullying, online harassment, and any type of Internet intimidation. _____

- engage with youth and fellow leaders in ways that allow us to build one another up, rather than demoralize, criticize, or demean. This includes the games we play and the jokes we share. _____

- be mindful and respectful of the safe spaces I create for youth.
  - I will avoid being alone with any youth behind closed doors, in a vehicle, or in any place where other adults are not present. _____
  - I will seek to encourage relationships and conversations in places of community that foster confidentiality, safety, and respect. _____

- respect and hold sacred the confidential information youth might share with me. However, I also covenant to operate within the boundaries of the law and will break confidences if legally required to do so. _____
  - I will establish healthy boundaries in my interactions with youth and other youth leaders. This includes dating and sharing personal experiences and friendships beyond the youth group or counseling relationship. _____

Printed Name _____ Date _____

Signature _____

(Each item above is to be initialed by the youth minister. The signed and dated document will be retained in the youth minister's record.)

Sample Authorization Form for Photo and Video Usage

I, _____ (printed name of legal parent or guardian), authorize [church name] to (please initial in the space provided after each bulleted item that you authorize):

- take pictures of my child to be posted inside the church. _____
- take pictures of my child for use in printed publications and on the church's website and social media accounts. _____
- include my child in videos that will be used for internal church purposes only (worship, internal communication, and invitation). _____
- include my child in videos that will be used on the church's website, social media, and YouTube accounts. _____

Signed:_____(parent or legal guardian)

Date: _____

(Retain this signed and dated document in the child's file.)

Sample Pastoral Ministry Covenant Regarding the Use of Facebook and Other Social Media

As a child of God, a member of the church universal, and a clergyperson in [church name], I covenant to use Facebook and other social media in ways that bring honor to God and show respect for self and for all others who might view my postings on Facebook and other social media.

In particular, I covenant to (initial in the space provided after you have read and agreed to each bulleted item):

- be cognizant of all that I post (in writing, images, and links) and its reflection on me as a Christian and a leader in the church. _____

- recognize and respect that my behaviors and actions are also a reflection on those who are the connectional system of The United Methodist Church. _____

- be mindful of the ways in which I offer personal information and how that affects my role and identity as a clergy leader and witness of Jesus Christ. _____

- take extra precautions to observe appropriate boundaries in my engagement in relationships online, both pastoral and personal. _____
    - with youth and children, this means _____
    - in establishing "friendships" with members of the congregation, this means _____

- take extra care not to be a hindrance to or cause harm to the pastor or the ministries of any church and congregation I have previously served. _____
    - I will not speak negatively or disparagingly about the current pastor or staff or the leadership they provide. _____
    - I will absolve myself of all pastoral responsibility and authority regarding any congregation I have previously served. _____
    - I will seek permission of the pastor currently appointed before officiating at weddings, funerals, baptisms, or in any formal leadership capacity related to members of former congregations. _____

- recognize and respect the privilege of utilizing social media as a tool for ministry. As such, I will regularly monitor the amount of time I spend on social media, the ways in which I am utilizing it, and its effects on my ministry and service in Christ's name. _____

Signed: _____ (Clergyperson)

Date: _____

Sources and Resources

Books and Publications

Anonymous. *Hope and Recovery: A Twelve-Step Guide for Healing from Compulsive Sexual Behavior.* Center City, MN: Hazelden, 1994.

Arterburn, Stephen, and Roger Marsh. *Internet Protect Your Kids.* Nashville: Integrity, 2007.

Bear, Euan. *Adults Molested as Children: A Survivor's Manual for Women and Men.* Orwell, VT: Safer Society Press, 1988.

Benyei, Candace R. *Understanding Clergy Misconduct in Religious Systems: Scapegoating, Family Secrets, and the Abuse of Power.* Binghamton, NY: Haworth, 1998.

Carnes, Patrick. *Out of the Shadows: Understanding Sexual Addiction.* Center City, MN: Hazelden, 1992.

Cloud, Henry, and John Townsend. *Boundaries: When to Say Yes, How to Say No to Take Control of Your Life.* Grand Rapids, MI: Zondervan, 1992.

———. *Boundaries in Dating: How Healthy Choices Grow Healthy Relationships.* Grand Rapids, MI: Zondervan, 2000.

Dawn, Marva J. *Sexual Character: Beyond Technique to Intimacy.* Grand Rapids, MI: Eerdmans, 1993.

Doehring, Carrie. *Taking Care: Monitoring Power Dynamics and Relational Boundaries in Pastoral Care and Counseling.* Nashville, TN: Abingdon, 1995.

Fassel, Diane. *Working Ourselves to Death: And the Rewards of Recovery.* San Francisco: HarperSanFrancisco, 1990.

Flynn, Nancy. *The E-Policy Handbook: Rules and Best Practices to Safely Manage Your Company's E-Mail, Blogs, Social Networking, and Other Electronic Communication Tools.* 2nd ed. Broadway, NY: American Management Association, 2009.

Fortune, Marie M. *Is Nothing Sacred? The Story of a Pastor, the Women He Sexually Abused, and the Congregation He Nearly Destroyed.* Cleveland, OH: United Church Press, 1999.

Notes

———. *Sexual Violence: The Unmentionable Sin.* Cleveland, OH: Pilgrim, 1983.

Fortune, Marie M., and James N. Poling. *Sexual Abuse by Clergy: A Crisis for the Church.* Decatur, GA: Journal of Pastoral Care, 1994.

Forward, Susan. *Emotional Blackmail: When the People in Your Life Use Fear, Obligation, and Guilt to Manipulate You.* New York: HarperCollins, 1997.

Friberg, Nils, and Mark R. Laaser. *Before the Fall: Preventing Pastoral Sexual Abuse.* Collegeville, MN: Liturgical Press, 1998.

Gaede, Beth Ann, ed. *When a Congregation Is Betrayed: Responding to Clergy Misconduct.* Herndon, VA: Alban Institute, 2005.

Gil, Eliana. *Outgrowing the Pain: A Book for and about Adults Abused as Children.* New York: Bantam, 1983.

Grenz, Stanley J., and Roy D. Bell. *Betrayal of Trust: Confronting and Preventing Clergy Sexual Misconduct.* 2nd ed. Grand Rapids: Baker, 2001.

GuideOne Center for Risk Management. *The Missing Ministry: Safety, Risk Management, and Protecting Your Church.* Loveland, CO: Group Publishing, 2008.

Gula, Richard M. *Ethics in Pastoral Ministry.* Mahwah, NJ: Paulist Press, 1996.

Hammar, Richard R. *Essential Guide to Copyright Law for Churches.* Carol Stream, IL: Christianity Today International, 2010.

———. *Pastor, Church, and Law,* 4th ed. Carol Stream, IL: Christianity Today International, 2007.

Hedges-Goettl, Len. *Sexual Abuse: Pastoral Responses.* Nashville, TN: Abingdon, 2004.

Hopkins, Nancy Myer, and Mark Laaser, eds. *Restoring the Soul of a Church: Healing Congregations Wounded by Clergy Sexual Misconduct.* Collegeville, MN: Liturgical Press, 1995.

Jones, L. Gregory. *Embodying Forgiveness: A Theological Analysis.* Grand Rapids, MI: Eerdmans, 1995.

Laaser, Mark R. *Healing the Wounds of Sexual Addiction.* Grand Rapids, MI: Zondervan, 1992.

McClintock, Karen A. *Preventing Sexual Abuse in Congregations: A Resource for Leaders.* Herndon, VA: Alban Institute, 2004.

Melton, Joy Thornburg. *Safe Sanctuaries for Ministers: Reducing the Risk of Abuse in the Church.* Nashville, TN: Discipleship Resources, 2009.

O'Briant, Paul. *Cybersafety for Families.* Nashville, TN: Discipleship Resources, 2010.

Ormerod, Neil, and Thea Ormerod. *When Ministers Sin: Sexual Abuse in the Churches.* Alexandria, Australia: Millennium, 1995.

Poling, James Newton. *The Abuse of Power: A Theological Problem.* Nashville, TN: Abingdon, 1991.

Sources and Resources

Poling, Nancy Werking, ed. *Victim to Survivor: Women Recovering from Clergy Sexual Abuse.* Cleveland, OH: United Church Press, 1999.

Ragsdale, Katherine Hancock, ed. *Boundary Wars: Intimacy and Distance in Healing Relationships.* Cleveland, OH: Pilgrim, 1996.

Rediger, G. Lloyd. *Beyond the Scandals: A Guide for Healthy Sexuality for Clergy.* Philadelphia, PA: Fortress, 2003.

Rutter, Peter. *Sex in the Forbidden Zone: When Men in Power—Therapists, Doctors, Clergy, Teachers, and Others—Betray Women's Trust.* New York: Fawcett, 1997.

Schneider, Jennifer, and Burt Schneider. *Sex, Lies, and Forgiveness: Couples Speaking Out on Healing from Sexual Addiction.* Center City, MN: Hazelden, 1991.

Schneider, Jennifer, and Robert Weiss. *Cybersex Exposed: Simple Fantasy or Obsession?* Center City, MN: Hazelden, 2001.

Sperry, Len. *Sex, Priestly Ministry, and the Church.* Collegeville, MN: Liturgical Press, 2003.

Thoburn, John, and Rob Baker, eds. *Clergy Sexual Misconduct: A Systems Approach to Prevention, Intervention, and Oversight.* Carefree, AZ: Gentle Path Press, 2011.

Thomas, Adam. *Digital Disciple: Real Christianity in a Virtual World.* Nashville, TN: Abingdon, 2011.

Turkle, Sherry. *Alone Together: Why We Expect More from Technology and Less from Each Other.* New York: Basic Books, 2011.

Wagner, Rachel, *Godwired: Religion, Ritual, and Virtual Reality.* New York: Routledge, 2012.

Willard, Nancy E. *Cyber-Safe Kids, Cyber-Savvy Teens: Helping Young People Learn to Use the Internet Safely and Responsibly.* San Francisco: Wiley, 2007.

Willimon, William H. *Pastor: A Reader for Ordained Ministry.* Nashville, TN: Abingdon, 2002.

Young, Mike. *Internet Laws: How to Protect Your Business Website Without a Lawyer.* CreateSpace Independent Publishing Platform, 2011.

Helpful Websites

Covering sexuality, religion, and misconduct issues:

FaithTrust Institute: http://www.faithtrustinstitute.org/news

General Commission on the Status and Role of Women: http://www.gcsrw.org; and www.umsexualethics.org

Religious Institute: http://religiousinstitute.org/news

Notes

Newsletters

The FaithTrust Institute offers an e-newsletter and e-mail reminders of trainings and webinars: http://www.faithtrustinstitute.org/subscribe

The General Commission on the Status and Role of Women offers a monthly newsletter via e-mail and online access (includes regular Sexual Ethics department): http://www.gcsrw.org/News/Followus.aspx

Blogs

Marie Fortune, "Marie's Blog," http://www.faithtrustinstitute.org/blog

> Rev. Dr. Marie Fortune, FaithTrust founder and senior analyst, offers analysis and commentary on issues that concern "working together to end sexual and domestic violence."

Debra Haffner, "Sexuality and Religion," http://www.religiousinstitute.org/sexuality-and-religion

> Rev. Debra W. Haffner is cofounder and executive director of the Religious Institute and an ordained Unitarian Universalist minister.

Jaime Romo, "Healing and Spirituality," http://www.jaimeromo.com/blog/archives/213

> "Dr. Jaime Romo is an educator, consultant, and author. He promotes healing from abuse and the prevention of child sexual abuse, particularly abuse by religious authorities or in the context of religious settings."

United Methodist Resources

The United Methodist Church law, policies, and procedures regarding clergy misconduct of a sexual nature are found primarily in the following places:

The Book of Discipline—2012:

¶¶ 341.5, 341.6, 362, 363, 364, and 2702

Social Principles ¶161, sections e, f, g, h, i

The Book of Resolutions—2012:

"Sexual Misconduct within Ministerial Relationships" (page 134)

"Eradication of Sexual Harassment in The United Methodist Church and Society" (page 141)

"Pornography and Sexual Violence" (page 155)

"Prevention of the Use of Pornography in the Church" (page 160)

"Reducing the Risk of Child Sexual Abuse in the Church" (page 240)

Sources and Resources

"Every Barrier Down: Toward Full Embrace of All Women in Church and Society" (page 494)

"Eradication of Sexism in the Church" (page 503)

"Church Participation by a Registered Sex Offender" (page 900)

The Evangelical Lutheran Church in America has resources similar to these in its *Constitution, Bylaws, and Continuing Resolutions* (www.elca.org).

The Presbyterian Church (PCUSA) has resources similar to these in its *Book of Order* (www.pcusa.org).

Notes

Notes

Chapter 1: Foundations and Pillars

1. *The United Methodist Hymnal* (Nashville: The United Methodist Publishing House, 1989), 44.

2. Steve Manskar, *Opening Ourselves to Grace: The Means of Grace and Discipleship* (Nashville: Discipleship Resources, 2006), 7.

Chapter 2: Application of Law to the Life of the Church

1. Richard R. Hammar, *Pastor, Church, and Law*, vol. 3, *Employment Law*, 4th ed. (Springfield, MA: Your Church Resources/Christianity Today, 2007), 31, §8-05.

Chapter 3: Basic Procedures for Ministry in a Virtual World

1. Pew Research Center's Internet and American Life Project Post-Election Survey, November 14–December 10, 2012; and Pew Research Center's Internet and American Life Project Omnibus Survey, December 13–16, 2012.

2. Nielsen and NM Incite, *How We Use Social Media: Highlights from the Social Media Report 2012*, December 12, 2012.

3. See Youtube.com/t/press_statistics.

4. Semiocast, "Geolocation and Activity Analysis of Pinterest Accounts by Semiocast," July 10, 2013, http://semiocast.com/en/publications/2013_07_10_Pinterest_has_70_million_users.

Chapter 4: Pornography and Obscenity

1. Adams Media Research, Forrester Research, Veronis Suhler Communications Industry Report, IVD.

2. Jerry Ropelato, "2005 and 2006 US Pornography Industry Revenue Statistics," TopTenREVIEWS, November 17, 2009, http://internet-filter-review.toptenreviews.com/internet-pornography-statistics.html.

Notes

3. Family Safe Media Statistics, quoted in "Internet Pornography: Facts and Figures," Alabama Policy Institute, December 3, 2009, http://www.alabamapolicyinstitute.org/issues/gti/issue.php?issueID=311&guideMainID=21.

4. "Enough Is Enough: Making the Internet Safe for Children and Families," Internet Safety 101, http://www.internetsafety101.org/abouteie.htm.

5. Ropelato, "2005 and 2006 US Pornography."

6. Janis Wolak, Kimberly Mitchell, and David Finkelhor, "Unwanted and Wanted Exposure to Online Pornography in a National Sample of Youth Internet Users," *Pediatrics* 119, no. 2 (2007): 247–57.

7. Benjamin Weiser, "Spelling It 'Dinsey,' Children on Web Got XXX," *New York Times*, September 4, 2003. http://www.nytimes.com/2003/09/04/nyregion/spelling-it-dinsey-children-on-web-got-xxx.html

8. Jill C. Manning, Senate testimony (Senate Committee on Judiciary, *Hearing on Pornography's Impact on Marriage and the Family: Subcommittee on the Constitution, Civil Rights, and Property Rights*), November 10, 2005, referencing J. Dedmon, "Is the Internet bad for your marriage? Online affairs, pornographic sites playing greater role in divorces," 2002, press release from American Academy of Matrimonial Lawyers.

9. Ibid.

10. Ropelato, "2005 and 2006 US Pornography."

11. Ibid.

12. Market Wired, "ChristiaNet Poll Finds That Evangelicals Are Addicted to Porn," August 7, 2006, http://www.marketwired.com/press-release/christianet-poll-finds-that-evangelicals-are-addicted-to-porn-703951.htm.

13. Ibid.

14. Ramona Richards, "Dirty Little Secret: Men Aren't the Only Ones Lured by Internet Porn," *Today's Christian Woman*, September/October 2003.

15. Marnie C. Ferree, *No Stones: Women Redeemed from Sexual Shame* (Fairfax, VA: Xulon Press, 2002), 62.

16. Richards, "Dirty Little Secret."

17. Thomas M. Santa, *Pornography* (Liguori, MO: Liguori Publications, n.d.), 14.

18. William M. Struthers, *Wired for Intimacy: How Pornography Hijacks the Male Brain* (Downers Grove, IL: InterVarsity Press, 2009).

19. Diana E. H. Russell, *Against Pornography: The Evidence of Harm* (Berkeley, CA: Russell Publications, 1993); and Manning, Senate testimony.

20. Dolf Zillmann, "Influence of Unrestrained Access to Erotica on Adolescents' and Young Adults' Dispositions toward Sexuality," *Journal of Adolescent Health* 27, no. 2 (August 2000) 41–44.

21. Hope and Healing Institute, 161 Ottawa NW, Grand Rapids, MI, http://www.hopeandhealingcenter.org/institute/.

22. "The Leadership Survey on Pastors and Internet Pornography," *Leadership Journal*, Winter 2001, http://www.christianitytoday.com/le/2001/winter/12.89.html?start=2.

23. "Social Principles: The Nurturing Community," *The Book of Discipline of The United Methodist Church—2008*. Copyright © 2008 by The United Methodist Publishing House; ¶161f. Used by permission.

24. Ibid., ¶161h.

25. Ibid., ¶2702.1, 3; and "Prevention of the Use of Pornography in the Church," in *The Book of Resolutions of The United Methodist Church—2008*. Copyright © 2008 by The United Methodist Publishing House. Used by permission.

 # About the Authors

Joy Thornburg Melton is an attorney and an ordained clergyperson in The United Methodist Church. She is a founding partner of Hindson & Melton, LLC, located in Atlanta, Georgia. Reverend Melton is a graduate of Pfeiffer University, Scarritt College, and Emory University Law School. She is a trustee of Pfeiffer University and serves as secretary of the Board of Trustees of Lake Junaluska Assembly. She also serves on the Sexual Ethics Task Force for the General Commission on the Status and Role of Women of The United Methodist Church. Reverend Melton has devoted her law practice and ministry to the protection of vulnerable individuals—children, youth, and older adults. She is the author of the Safe Sanctuaries series of resources, the foundational studies widely used by United Methodist and other Christian churches to design ministries with children, youth, and older adults. In her law practice, Reverend Melton works closely with churches, both small and large, to structure employment and operational procedures that will provide good stewardship of the church's resources and strengthen the church's ministry.

Michelle L. Foster is an ordained deacon in The United Methodist Church. She is a member of the Western North Carolina Conference and currently resides in High Point, North Carolina, where she serves on a clergy team in a local congregation. Additionally, Reverend Foster serves as the WNCC Coordinator of Clergy Ethics, the chair of the Order of Deacons, and as a member of the Western North Carolina Conference Board of Ordained Ministry. In addition to her local church and conference work, Reverend Foster also serves on the Sexual Ethics Task Force for the General Commission on the Status and Role of Women of The United Methodist Church. She is a graduate of Greensboro College and Perkins School of Theology at Southern Methodist University. Gifted in the areas of Christian education and church leadership ethics, Reverend Foster has devoted her ministry to leading, equipping, and encouraging healthy leaders and healthy communities where all of God's children can worship, grow, frolic, and contemplate the journey toward faithful discipleship in Jesus' name.

CPSIA information can be obtained at www.ICGtesting.com
Printed in the USA
LVOW10s2050130814

399018LV00003B/10/P